STRANGE UNUSUAL GROSS & COOL ANIMALS

For Charlotte & Christopher

A special thanks to Beth Sutinis and Deirdre Langeland for inviting me on this safari with them into the rare and wonderful world known as the Animal Planet

To Laura Tucker and her fearless band of brave librarians at the Homewood Public Library

And to Debra Ghigna, my beloved editor-in-residence

LIBERTY
STREET

Executive Editor: Beth Sutinis
Project editor: Deirdre Langeland
Art director: Georgia Morrissey
Designer: Dirk Kaufman
Photo researcher: Nataki Hewling
Production manager: Susan Chodakiewicz
Indexing: Wendy Allex
Prepress imaging: Dirk Kaufman and Andrij Borys Associates, LLC

Published by Liberty Street, an imprint of Time Inc. Books
225 Liberty Street
New York, New York 10281

LIBERTY STREET is a trademark of Time Inc.

ISBN 10: 1-61893-166-0
ISBN 13: 978-1-61893-166-5
Library of Congress Control Number: 2016939212

First edition, 2016

1 TLF 16

10 9 8 7 6 5 4 3 2 1

Time Inc. Books products may be purchased for business or promotional use. For information on bulk purchases, please contact Christi Crowley in the Special Sales Department at (845) 895-9858.

To order Time Inc. Books Collector's Editions, please call (800) 327-6388, Monday through Friday, 7 a.m. to 9 p.m., Central Time.

We welcome your comments and suggestions about Time Inc. Books. Please write to us at:
Time Inc. Books

Attention: Book Editors

P.O. Box 62310
Tampa, Florida 33662-2310

timeincbooks.com

Half title page: Leaf mimic katydid
Title page: Hammerhead shark

SPHYNX

Unlike wild animals, such as the naked mole rat, that have evolved without fur to be better adapted to their environment, the sphynx cat is bald as a result of selective breeding.

ANIMAL PLANET

STRANGE UNUSUAL GROSS & COOL ANIMALS

Charles Ghigna

CONTENTS

INTRODUCTION

The world is full of incredible creatures, each one a wonderful oddity.

Some are weird. Some are scary. And some are just disgusting!

This is a book of a few of the world's most amazing animals. From the tiny sea angel to the gigantic blue whale, these are the strange, unusual, gross, and cool creatures that crawl, fly, and swim across planet Earth.

Come in and take a look—if you dare!

ABOUT THIS BOOK

Throughout this book, you will find four different types of pages. Follow the tabs on the right side of the book to jump to the one you want to read.

GALLERY spreads explore a theme, introducing you to several animals that live in different parts of the world but are adapted to their environments in similar ways.

FEATURED CREATURE pages let you get to know one extraordinary animal through detailed descriptions of its life, stat boxes, and maps that show where the animal lives.

CREATURE COLLECTION spreads bring together a big group of animals to compare, contrast, and learn more about.

MACROVIEW pages show tiny details of very small animals through gorgeous macrophotographs.

NUDIBRANCH

STRANGE HOW WE AS HUMANS
VIEW CREATURES GREAT AND SMALL—
FOR WE WHO SEE THEIR STRANGENESS
ARE THE STRANGEST ONES OF ALL!

CREATURES OF THE DEEP

Flexible body is buoyant in deep water.

Small pectoral fin

DEEP SEA OCTOPOD
FOUND UP TO 2,000 FEET (600 M)

This small cephalopod can fit in a human hand. It's hardy, though, living three times as long as its shallow-water cousins.

Blobfish
VOTED THE WORLD'S UGLIEST ANIMAL IN 2013

The blobfish lives on the bottom of the sea. It has almost no muscles and doesn't swim. It bobs along the ocean floor off the coasts of Australia, New Zealand, and Tasmania at depths of up to 4,000 feet. Even though it lays more than 9,000 eggs at a time, it is in danger of extinction.

FANGTOOTH
FOUND UP TO 16,500 FEET (5,000 M)

The fangtooth's teeth are so large it can never close its mouth. During the day the fangtooth stays as deep as 16,500 feet. In the evening it swims up to feed. It is one of the few fish that rely on a sense of smell to find prey.

FRILLED SHARK

FOUND UP TO 5,000 FEET (1,500 M)

The frilled shark looks like an eel—if an eel had 25 rows of 300 triangular-shaped, needle-sharp teeth! Those chompers are perfect for taking apart slippery cephalopods such as cuttlefish, octopuses, and squid. One superfreaky aspect of this fish's anatomy is that its mouth continues to the rear of its head, where it joins up with the six frilled gills that give it its name.

OCEAN SURFACE

EPIPELAGIC ZONE

200 M

MESOPELAGIC ZONE

1,000 M

GALLERY

The ocean is divided into zones that decrease in light and heat and increase in pressure as you travel from the surface to the ocean floor—and beyond.

BATHYPELAGIC ZONE

VAMPIRE SQUID

FOUND UP TO 3,200 FEET (1,000 M)

The vampire squid has large fins at the top of its body that resemble ears. When it is frightened, the vampire squid can squirt a cloud of glowing mucus into the water around it.

4,000 M

Each tooth has three points, like a trident.

HUMPBACK ANGLERFISH

FOUND UP TO 9,800 FEET (3,000 M)

This anglerfish lives more than a mile deep in the dark ocean, where it uses its bioluminescent lure to attract prey.

ABYSSOPELAGIC ZONE

SNIPE EEL

FOUND UP TO 13,000 FEET (4,000 M)

A five-foot-long snipe eel weighs only a few ounces. It has a birdlike beak with a curved tip. The beak is covered with tiny hook teeth used to entangle tasty shrimp.

OCEAN FLOOR

HADOPELAGIC ZONE

STAR-NOSED MOLE

The star-nosed mole is a talented creature. Its nose is covered in 22 sensitive appendages that are so good at detecting vibrations they can tell when earthquakes are coming. The star-nosed mole is also an excellent swimmer. It can even smell underwater by blowing bubbles it then breathes in through its nose. It lives in wet lowland areas and uses its sensitive nose to seek out dinner: worms, insects, mollusks, and small fish that it finds at the bottoms of lakes, ponds, and streams. While star-nosed moles can judge light intensity, they are mostly blind, which has its hazards. They are often eaten by hawks, owls, foxes, weasels, minks, and skunks.

Blackish-brown fur is water-repellent, perfect for a creature that hides its burrow entrance below the waterline.

Meet the World's most sensitive snout.

Large claws are ideal for digging tunnels.

NAKED MOLE RAT
FELLOW FREAKY BURROWER

Because the naked mole rat can see only light and shadow, it uses its whiskers to feel its way around. It lives underground in tunnel systems, usually with 75 to 80 other mole rats. One colony was found to have 290!

CREATURE FEATURES

Scientific Name
Condylura cristata

Class
Mammals

Length
7 to 7.5 inches (17 to 19 cm)

Weight
1.8 ounces (50 g)

Habitat
Marshes, wet meadows, and the banks of streams, lakes, and ponds

Home
Its tunnels are about 1.5 inches (4 cm) in diameter and 2 to 24 inches (5 to 60 cm) deep.

Diet
Leeches, snails, and small fish, as well as earthworms and centipedes

Range
Eastern Canada and United States

Conservation Status
Least Concern

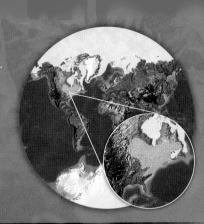

Tiny eyes don't do much. The mole is functionally blind.

Fleshy appendages pack five times more touch sensing than a human hand into an area that is smaller than a thumbprint.

Tweezer-like front teeth make short work of tiny invertebrates, the mole's favorite foods.

STRANGE BIRDS

 IMPERIAL SHAG

▶ Waters of South America and Sub Antarctic
This swimming bird has heavy bones that help it dive up to 80 feet in pursuit of fish.

 BLACK-WINGED STILT

▶ Wetlands throughout Africa and Eurasia
More than half of this bird's height comes from its legs, which allow it to wade in deep water.

 ANDEAN COCK-OF-THE-ROCK

▶ Cloud forests in western South America
Its crest makes this bird appear strangely shaped, but the crest is all feathers.

 COMMON POTOO

▶ Rain forests of northern South America
Giant eyes make for better night vision—and give this bird a very unusual look.

AMERICAN FLAMINGO

Beta-carotene from the shells of shrimp and other crustaceans the bird eats gives the flamingo its pink color.

SOUTHERN GROUND HORNBILL

▶ Woodlands and savannas in southern Africa
Folds of skin around this hornbill's eyes help to protect them from dust.

 ## VICTORIA'S RIFLEBIRD

▶ Forests in northeastern Australia
The male riflebird raises his wings in a circle and sways from side to side to attract mates.

 ## SOUTHERN ROCKHOPPER PENGUIN

▶ Waters of South America and Sub Antarctic
This penguin earns its name by hopping from rock to rock, rather than waddling.

 ## COMMON OSTRICH

▶ Grasslands and semi-deserts across Africa
Ostriches may not be able to fly, but they can run up to 40 miles per hour!

 ## DEMOISELLE CRANE

▶ Grasslands near water in central Asia
Flocks of this long-legged bird can number in the thousands, and sometimes the tens of thousands!

 ## HELMETED GUINEA FOWL

▶ Bushlands and savannas across Africa
The guinea fowl can only fly for short bursts, but it finds safety in numbers, living in large flocks.

 ## CALIFORNIA CONDOR

▶ Scrublands and savannas in western North America
The condor was nearly extinct in the 1980s. Thanks to conservation measures, the population is on the rise.

 ## SCARLET IBIS

▶ Wetlands in northern South America
The long bill of this brightly colored marsh bird is perfect for poking in the mud in search of food.

 ## SHOEBILL

▶ Wetlands in central Africa
This wader is well adapted to its swampy home and will even nest on islands made of floating plants!

RED-LIPPED BATFISH

The red-lipped batfish is found in the waters around the Galápagos Islands, where Charles Darwin developed his theory of evolution more than 150 years ago. No doubt, Darwin would have been fascinated by the ways in which this fish has evolved to live in its home. Shaped like a bat in flight, it has a very strange way of getting around—it uses its pectoral fins to walk across the ocean floor. In fact, it's a terrible swimmer. Visitors to the deep waters of the Pacific Ocean needn't worry. Though this batfish may look alarming, it is completely harmless—unless you're a shrimp.

Mottled color helps the fish blend in with the sandy ocean floor.

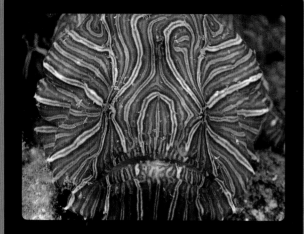

PSYCHEDELIC FROGFISH

ANOTHER SAND WALKER

Instead of swimming, this fish uses jet propulsion to get around. It walks along the seafloor on its pectoral fins, shoots water through its gills, and pushes off from the bottom like a bouncing ball. The psychedelic frogfish is also called the psychedelica.

The fish uses its unusual pectoral fins to "walk" along the ocean floor.

As a batfish matures, the "horn" on its forehead grows into a long spine, most likely used for luring prey.

Have you ever heard of a fish that can't swim?

No one is sure why the batfish has bright red lips—it may be a way to attract mates.

CREATURE FEATURES

Scientific Name
Ogcocephalus darwini

Class
Ray-finned fishes

Length
Up to 8 inches (20 cm)

Habitat
Sandy bottoms near reefs, at depths of 10 to 250 feet (3 to 76 m), more common at depths of more than 32 feet (10 m)

Diet
Prefers to eat small invertebrates, such as worms, crabs, and mollusks, that can be found on the ocean floor

Range
Pacific Ocean, in the waters surrounding the Galápagos Islands

Conservation Status
Least Concern

RED-EYED CROCODILE SKINK

The red-eyed crocodile skink may look like a tiny crocodile, but it rarely bites. It is very shy and spends most of its time hiding under leaves and shrubs, coming out only during the early morning and late afternoon. Males are territorial and will fight with other males for mates. The female skink lays one egg at a time and guards it until it hatches. All skinks make a squeaky croaking sound when they are in trouble, and freeze and faint when they are frightened.

Do not sneak up behind a skink and yell "BOO!"

Four rows of pointed spines on its back look like the ridges on a crocodile.

MYOTONIC GOAT
FELLOW FAINTER

This goat might look very different from a skink, but the two animals have one big thing in common. When startled, myotonic goats stiffen and will often fall over. The goats aren't really fainting. Instead, their legs become immobile, causing them to lose their balance and appear to faint.

CREATURE FEATURES

Scientific Name
Tribolonotus gracilis

Class
Reptiles

Length
Up to 10 inches (25 cm)

Habitat
Tropical rain forests

Diet
Small invertebrates such as worms, beetles, and crickets

Range
Indonesia and the island of New Guinea

Conservation Status
Least Concern

Six bony points make the skink look much fiercer than it is.

Rosy circles around its eyes give this skink its name.

FEATURED CREATURE

RUSTY TUSSOCK MOTH

THAT'S SCENTS-IBLE!

The feathery antennae on this European moth might look decorative, but they're loaded with special smell receptors that can detect the scent of a female.

LOWLAND STREAKED TENREC

The island of Madagascar, off the coast of Africa, is home to 31 kinds of tenrec. They all evolved from one ancestor into very different animals, each occupying its own habitat on the island. The lowland streaked tenrec looks a bit like a tiny, hairy hedgehog. Family groups live together in underground burrows. They stay in close contact while they forage for food on the forest floor, clicking their tongues and using *stridulation*, rubbing special quills on their backs together to create ultrasonic vibrations. The lowland streaked tenrec—along with its close cousin the highland streaked tenrec—is the only mammal known to stridulate.

Bold yellow stripes distinguish this species from other types of tenrec.

A tiny, prickly musician.

When threatened, the tenrec will meet its enemy head-on, facing them with the detachable, barbed quills on its head.

Spines on the tenrec's back can be rubbed together to make noises that are too high for humans to hear.

The long snout is perfect for rooting under leaves in search of worms.

CREATURE FEATURES

Scientific Name
Hemicentetes semispinosus

Class
Mammals

Length
Up to 7.5 inches (19 cm)

Weight
Up to 7 ounces (200 g)

Habitat
Tropical rain forest. Up to 20 family members share a burrow 5 feet (1.5 m) long and 6 inches (15 cm) deep.

Diet
Small invertebrates, especially worms

Range
The eastern and northern parts of Madagascar

Conservation Status
Least Concern

BETIC MIDWIFE TOAD

The Betic midwife toad has one of the most unusual breeding behaviors of any animal in the world. After the female lays a string of eggs, the male wraps them around his hind legs and carries them until they are ready to hatch. He then deposits them in a pool of water, where the tadpoles remain for up to a year. The toad has small warts on his back that give off a strong-smelling poison when he is handled or attacked. The powerful poison wards off predators and protects the eggs that he carries. *What a good daddy!*

Smooth, shiny skin is mottled to blend in with pebbles and leaves on the forest floor.

Eggs ride on their father's hind legs until they are ready to hatch.

CREATURE FEATURES

Scientific Name
Alytes dickhilleni

Class
Amphibians

Length
Up to 1 inch (2.5 cm)

Weight
Up to 7 ounces (200 g)

Habitat
Temperate mountain forests

Home
Hides during the day under stones and logs, or in a burrow dug in sandy soil

Diet
Adults eat beetles, crickets, flies, caterpillars, centipedes, and millipedes. Tadpoles feed on vegetable matter.

Range
Lives more than a mile up in the mountains of southeastern Spain

Conservation Status
Vulnerable

White bumps contain a stinky poison that keeps predators away.

Vertical pupils allow the toad to follow the movement of prey, even in the dark.

Babies on board!

DARWIN'S FROG

FELLOW FREAKY FATHER

The Darwin's frog lives in the forest streams of Chile and Argentina, South America. It has an unusual birth. After the eggs develop into embryos and begin to move, the male frog swallows the tadpoles and holds them in his vocal sac. When the tadpoles turn into froglets, they hop out of their father's mouth.

CREATURES OF THE DESERT

RED KANGAROO

THE LARGEST OF ALL KANGAROOS

This Australian native can grow up to 6 feet tall and weigh more than 200 pounds! The position of its eyes allows it to see 325° around its body—almost a complete circle.

DESERT TORTOISE

AN HERBIVORE

This North American turtle lives up to 80 years and eats grasses, herbs, wildflowers, and cacti. It spends more than 95% of its life underground in burrows.

CACTUS WREN

SMART AND CURIOUS

This small bird nests in cactus plants, where it is protected by prickly cactus spines. Its curiosity often gets it into trouble when it flies into cars and homes with open windows or doors.

COYOTE

SWIFT COUSIN OF THE WOLF

This smaller cousin of the gray wolf and the jackal can run up to 40 miles an hour. It has keen vision and a strong sense of smell, and can be heard howling when alone, especially at night.

Flic-Flac Spider

TINY ACROBAT

This very unusual huntsman spider was recently discovered in Morocco. To escape from its predators, it doubles its speed by using forward and backward flips. It is nocturnal and spends the hot daylight hours in an underground burrow.

Horns can grow up to 3 feet long.

DESERT BIGHORN SHEEP

STRONG AND FIERCE

The ram of this species can weigh up to 200 pounds and has been known to battle with other rams nonstop for hours. It can go for days without drinking water. When it is thirsty, it breaks open cacti with its horns.

Hooves are adapted to grip small bumps in the terrain, so the sheep can climb.

BANDED GILA MONSTER

VENOMOUS LIZARD

This giant, slow-moving lizard can bite quickly and hold on tight. The good news: It spends 90% of its time underground.

25

PROBOSCIS MONKEY

Proboscis monkeys are born with black fur and blue faces, but as they grow, their fur turns reddish brown and their faces pink-orange. They may look strange to humans, but every part of their bodies helps them survive in the rain forest. The males use their noses to amplify their calls so that they can be heard from far away. Proboscis monkeys have partially webbed feet and are very good swimmers. They can sometimes swim faster than crocodilians, such as the false gavial, which have been known to enjoy the occasional proboscis monkey snack. They can even swim underwater for up to 60 feet! Because their rain forest home is being destroyed, the proboscis monkey is an endangered species.

Big nose, big belly...
really big advantage.

CREATURE FEATURES

Scientific Name
Nasalis larvatus

Class
Mammals

Length
Males up to 3 feet (90 cm) tall;
females up to 2 feet (62 cm) tall

Weight
Males up to 44 pounds (20 kg);
females up to 22 pounds (10 kg)

Habitat
Trees in forests and swamps

Home
Spends most of its life in trees, only traveling on the ground when it is unavoidable

Diet
Leaves and unripe fruit, occasionally seeds and insects

Range
The island of Borneo

Conservation Status
Endangered

Fur is black in infants and turns reddish brown as the animal matures.

Females have smaller noses than their mates.

A large stomach full of bacteria digests tough cellulose from plants and gives the monkey a distinct potbelly.

A long tail helps balance the monkey while leaping and climbing.

Partially webbed feet make for speedy swimming.

The large nose of the male monkey amplifies calls, which attract mates and scare off other males.

27

RHOMBIC EGG EATER

The rhombic egg eater does not have a venomous bite. In fact, it hardly has any teeth. It is an excellent climber—a useful skill in a creature that lives entirely on a diet of bird eggs. Its keen sense of smell lets it know whether an egg is rotten or good to eat. Its neck and jaws are very flexible, and it can eat eggs that are larger than its head. Once it has an egg in its mouth, the snake flexes its muscles, crushes the shell, squeezes the liquid out of the egg, and regurgitates the entire crushed eggshell. When threatened, it puts on an impressive display, rubbing its scales together quickly and making a rasping noise that sounds like hissing. It lunges like a venomous snake that is ready to strike.

Bony protrusions inside the snake's spine break the egg after it is swallowed.

DRAGON SNAKE

FELLOW SELECTIVE SLITHERER

The dragon snake is also a picky eater. It lives in Thailand, Myanmar, and Indonesia, where it comes out at night to search for its favorite prey—frogs. The dragon snake is not smooth like other snakes. It has three rows of ridges running down its back like a mythical dragon.

Scientific Name
Dasypeltis scabra

Class
Reptiles

Length
More than 3 feet (90 cm)

Habitat
Although mainly a savanna species, it inhabits most biomes, except desert.

Home
Spends most of its time on the ground, but can climb trees to reach bird nests

Diet
Bird eggs

Range
Africa and the Arabian Peninsula

Conservation Status
Least Concern

Don't tell anyone—it only LOOKS dangerous.

Large jaws enable it to eat eggs that are bigger than its head.

The tongue is used to "smell" eggs before they are eaten to ensure that they are fresh.

CREATURES OF THE NIGHT

Teeth grow continuously.

Sloths are mostly nearsighted.

SKUNK

BEAUTIFUL AND FOUL

Its fur is black and white with a thick white stripe running from its snout to its forehead. It is the size of an average house cat and is friendly—unless it is threatened!

Sloths are so slow-moving that algae grow in their fur.

FAT-TAILED SCORPION

FAST AND AGGRESSIVE

This arachnid can go months without food, but when it gets hungry, it captures prey and crushes it with its pincers while injecting venom and paralyzing the victim. It eats insects, spiders, lizards, and small mice.

TWO-TOED SLOTH

SLOW AND STEADY

A slow-moving climber, the sloth spends most of its life hanging upside down in trees, and uses its long, curved claws to move along branches with a hand-over-hand motion. Though it crawls slowly on the ground, it is a very good swimmer!

Black Rhinoceros

TWO-HORNED LONER

The black rhino has two horns that can grow over 4 feet long! It spends most of its time alone and relies on its sharp hearing and keen sense of smell to find other rhinos.

TARANTULA

HAIRY AND HARMLESS

Because of its big, hairy body, most people are afraid of the tarantula, but tarantulas usually avoid humans. Its mild venom is less potent than a bee sting.

The eyes are the largest, in proportion to its body, of any mammal.

Ears can pick up ultrasonic frequencies.

TARSIER

LITTLE BIG-EYED MONKEY

This tiny primate has eyes the size of its brain! It has superlong fingers and can leap 40 times its body length! It mostly uses its amazing abilities to catch insects. The Horsfield's tarsier even eats birds and bats!

AARDVARK

MOST UNUSUAL ANIMAL

The aardvark has ears like a rabbit's, feet like a duck's, claws like a bear's, a tail like a kangaroo's, and a tongue like an anteater's. Yet it does not belong to any of these species.

ROSY WOLFSNAIL

The rosy wolfsnail has a beautiful rose-colored shell. But do not let that fool you. The wolfsnail is a cannibal! It moves three times faster than other snails. It sneaks up behind them and devours them. *Gotcha!* When the wolfsnail finds another snail's slime trail, it carefully follows the path to its prey. After it eats the smaller snail, all that remains is an empty shell. If the other snail is very small, the wolfsnail swallows it whole, shell and all. In 1955, the wolfsnail was brought to Hawaii to help control the population of the giant African land snail. Instead, the wolfsnail began attacking native snails, causing entire species, such as the little Oahu tree snail, to become extinct.

Like all land snails, wolfsnails breathe through a pore in their mantle.

Eyestalks can be pulled back into the body for protection.

Tentacles feel the ground and help the snail orient itself.

Extralong esophagus extends out of the snail's mouth while sharp radula pulls prey from its shell.

Don't let its pretty shell fool you.

A hard shell protects the snail from predators.

CREATURE FEATURES

Scientific Name
Euglandina rosea

Class
Gastropods

Length
Shell can be as long as 3 inches
(7 cm)

Habitat
Tropical and subtropical forests, gardens,
and lawns

Home
Leaf litter and loose soil

Diet
Snails and slugs

Range
Native to the southeastern United States;
introduced to Hawaii and other islands

Conservation Status
Alien Invader

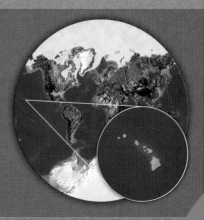

MIMICS

The insect's eyes are close in color to its body.

Ridges on the wings mimic the veins of leaves.

LEAF INSECT

LIKES TO BE *LEAFED* ALONE

The flat, veiny wings of this rain forest insect look just like leaves, allowing it to hide in plain sight.

MEXICAN MILK SNAKE

ALL BARK AND NO BITE

areas where milk snakes live, you can also find al snakes. That deadly species is red, black, and yellow, and the less milk snake keeps safe by sporting similar colors.

Ant

Ant mimic spider

HUMMINGBIRD MOTH
HIDES WHILE HOVERING

It hums and hovers just like a hummingbird does, but this visitor to North American flower gardens isn't a bird—it's a moth. Looking like a bird means this insect *doesn't* look like something that other birds, its main predators, would want to eat.

ANT MIMIC SPIDER
SAFETY IN NUMBERS

Most predators can tell a tasty spider from a less-than-tasty, possibly stinging ant—but not if the spider is really good at pretending. Ant mimic spiders have thinner waists than other spider species. They hold their front legs up in the air to look like antennae, too. Some ant mimic spiders even use this trick to sneak up on ants and eat them!

Mimic Octopus
MASTER OF DISGUISE

This ocean-dweller can change its color, and even its shape, to mimic more dangerous sea creatures such as sea snakes, flatfish, and lionfish. If that fails, it will squirt a confusing cloud of ink into the water around it and make its escape.

TONKIN BUG-EYED FROG
MOSSY ROCK HOPPER

This bumpy frog spends most of its time in damp caves and on rocky cliffs in the Vietnamese rain forest, where looking like a patch of moss is a great way to hide. When threatened, it curls into a ball and stays perfectly still, hoping its attacker will mistake it for a plant.

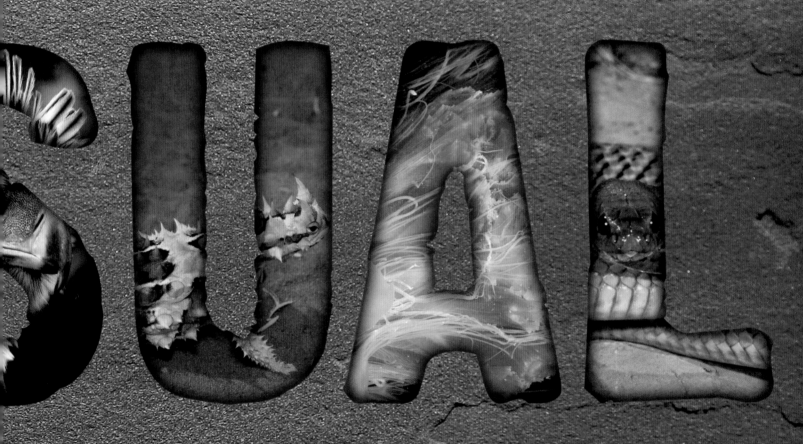

UNUSUAL IS WHAT WE CALL
THE WEIRD, THE FAST, THE RARE.
WE CLASSIFY EACH CREATURE—
BUT DO THEY REALLY CARE?

MALEO

The maleo is a peculiar-looking bird, with a yellow face, red eyes, an orange beak, and a dark gray crown that looks like a helmet. They are also unusually faithful. Once maleos mate, they stay together for the rest of their lives. But they don't show the same devotion to their chicks. When a maleo hen is ready to lay an egg, the parents travel to a communal nesting ground, where they dig a hole in the sand, carefully checking the temperature until they find a spot warmed by the sun or geothermal activity to a temperature of 91 degrees Fahrenheit. The female lays one giant egg—five times as large as a chicken egg— covers it in sand, then leaves it behind. Lucky for the maleo chick, it is able to fly as soon as it hatches. *That would be like a human baby being able to walk as soon as he or she is born!*

Grayish-blue feet have four long, slightly webbed toes that are ideal for digging nest holes in the sand.

CREATURE FEATURES

Scientific Name
Macrocephalon maleo

Class
Birds

Length
Up to 2 feet (61 cm)

Habitat
Rain forests in lowlands and on hillsides, up to 3,280 feet (1 km)

Home
Searches the forest floor for food during the day, roosts in trees at night

Diet
Fruit, seeds, small insects, and mollusks

Range
The island of Sulawesi in Indonesia

Conservation Status
Endangered

The horn has hollow pockets, supported by bony struts. Some think it might absorb vibrations created when the maleo pecks at hard nuts.

A strong beak is perfect for opening nuts and seeds.

This baby can fly!

MALEO CHICK
JUST HATCHED

When the chick hatches, it has a big job ahead of it. It has to dig its way out of a nest that could be as much as 3 feet deep—a job that can take as long as two days. That's a lot of digging for a newborn!

INLAND TAIPAN

The inland taipan is by far the most venomous land snake on the planet. It is extremely fast and can strike instantly and accurately, delivering up to eight venomous bites in one single attack. One bite from it is enough to kill 100 humans or 250,000 mice. The good news: It is shy and likes to be left alone. In fact, there isn't a single recorded case of a human being killed by one. But it will defend itself if it needs to. Despite its powerful bite, the inland taipan has two predators: the king brown snake and the perentie monitor lizard.

Round pupils are perfect for foraging in daylight.

The most venomous snake in the world.

Ventral scales move the snake forward.

The snake's color changes depending on the season. The darker color in winter helps the snake stay warm when temperatures drop.

RHINOCEROS VIPER

SIMILAR STRIKER

The rhinoceros viper is considered one of the most beautiful and dangerous snakes in the world. It can move forward or sideways and strike quickly without coiling. A small amount of its venom can kill. As if that weren't enough, the rhinoceros viper has more than 40 rows of sharp dorsal scales.

Smooth dorsal scales protect against cuts and moisture loss.

CREATURE FEATURES

Scientific Name
Oxyuranus microlepidotus

Class
Reptiles

Length
Up to 8 feet (2.5 m)

Life Span
Up to 20 years

Habitat
Dried floodplains, rocky outcroppings in semi-arid regions

Home
Prefers to hide in the deep cracks created when floodplains dry, can also be found under and around rock formations

Diet
Mice and rats

Range
Central-East Australia

Conservation Status
Least Concern

MARVELOUS MAMMALS

LONG-EARED JERBOA
▸ **Deserts in China and Mongolia**
This insectivore's large ears help keep it cool and pick up the sound of approaching predators.

GOLDEN-CROWNED SIFAKA
▸ **Forests in northeastern Madagascar**
This lemur is critically endangered because slash-and-burn farming is destroying its forest home.

HOODED SEAL
▸ **Sea ice and waters of the North Atlantic**
To attract mates, the male hooded seal blows air into a special sac that bulges from his nose.

MALAYAN TAPIR
▸ **Rain forests of Malaysia and Thailand**
The tapir can bend its flexible nose to use it as a snorkel while swimming.

MANDRILL
The colorful face of a male mandrill signals his dominance in the group and helps attract mates. The mandrill is the largest species of monkey.

MANED WOLF

▶ **Grasslands in eastern South America**
The extralong legs of this wolf raise it above tall grass so that it can see over long distances.

 PINK FAIRY ARMADILLO

▶ **Grasslands and sandy plains in Argentina**
The smallest of all armadillos, this tiny tunneler can dig a hole big enough to bury itself in seconds.

 AYE-AYE

▶ **Forests in eastern Madagascar**
This endangered primate, with its big eyes and ears, and long, slender fingers, is built for night climbing

 HISPANIOLAN SOLENODON

▶ **Forests in Haiti and the Dominican Republic**
The solenodon family evolved away from other mammals 76 million years ago.

 ENGLISH LONGHORN CATTLE

▶ **Northern England**
This large animal was once used to pull carts. Males weigh an average of 2,000 pounds.

 YANGTZE RIVER DOLPHIN

▶ **The Yangtze river in China**
Conservationists fear this dolphin may be extinct. None have been seen since 2001.

 BLUE WHALE

▶ **Every ocean in the world**
This whale is the largest animal to ever live on Earth—even bigger than the biggest dinosaur!

 GHOST BAT

▶ **Arid zones in northern Australia**
This flying mammal has especially thin skin on its wings, which gives it a ghostly look at night.

 BALD UAKARI

▶ **Floodplain forests of Brazil and Peru**
The thin skin of this monkey's face lacks pigment, allowing others to see the blood underneath.

COELACANTH

For many years, the coelacanth was thought to be extinct. The only traces of it were fossils dating back millions of years—until one was caught in 1938. During the day, the well-fed coelacanth sleeps in a cave at the bottom of the ocean. At night, it swims by drifting along with the current, looking for smaller fish to eat. Unlike most other fish, the coelacanth hatches from an egg inside its mother, making it one of the only species of fish to experience a live birth. The mother and father coelacanth only mate with each other. Because of its large size, the coelacanth has few predators.

The coelacanth does not have vertebrae like other fish. Instead, it has a tube filled with oil, called a *notochord*.

An intracranial joint allows the fish to open its mouth wide and swallow prey whole.

Large eyes are adapted to seeing in the near-dark.

Rows of sharp teeth on its upper and lower jaw keep prey from escaping once they have been caught.

Did it really come back from the dead?

CREATURE FEATURES

Scientific Name
Latimeria chalumnae

Class
Lobe-finned fish

Length
Up to 6 feet (2 meters)

Weight
More than 200 pounds (91 kg)

Life Span
More than 60 years

Habitat
Temperate water off volcanic islands,
500 to 800 feet (152 to 244 m) deep

Home
Underwater caves

Diet
Smaller fish

Range
Indian Ocean, near the Comoro Islands off
the east coast of Africa

Conservation Status
Critically Endangered

Lobed fins sit on stalks, rather
than being attached directly to
the body, and resemble the legs
of prehistoric land animals.

LAOTIAN ROCK RAT

FELLOW FOSSIL

The Laotian rock rat was discovered in 1996 in Laos.
Scientists found the unusual animal in a meat market.
They later realized that the rock rat is the only surviving
species from a family of mammals that went extinct
11 million years ago! Even the rock rats may not be
around for much longer. They are endangered and
their numbers continue to decline.

KAKAPO

The kakapo lives in the forests of New Zealand. Its name comes from two Maori words, *kaka*, meaning "parrot," and *po* meaning "night." It is the heaviest parrot on the planet and the only parrot that does not fly. Don't feel sorry for the kakapo, though. It is an excellent runner and climber. It sometimes climbs tall trees, then spreads its wings and parachutes down. This helps the parrot escape from predators such as cats, rats, ferrets, and weasels. If it is lucky, the kakapo has one of the longest life spans of any bird—nearly 100 years! Even so, the kakapo is critically endangered, with just 126 birds still living in the wild.

Now, that's an old bird!

Strong legs and large feet make the parrot a good climber.

CREATURE FEATURES

Scientific Name
Strigops habroptilus

Class
Birds

Length
Up to 2 feet (60 cm)

Weight
Up to 5 pounds (2 kg)

Life Span
Up to 100 years

Habitat
Forests

Diet
Plants, seeds, and fruit

Range
New Zealand

Conservation Status
Critically Endangered

Yellow, green, and brown feathers help the parrot blend in with plants and leaf litter on the forest floor.

The wings aren't large enough for flight, but they make a decent parachute for leaping out of trees as high as 17 feet.

Feathers arranged in a disk shape around the bird's face help focus sound.

A strong beak with a sharp lower mandible cracks nuts and seeds and breaks into tough plants.

RHINOCEROS HORNBILL
ANOTHER ELDERLY BIRD

The rhinoceros hornbill is another one of the longest-living birds in the world, surviving up to 90 years! When the female starts to lay eggs, she works with her mate to seal herself into a hole in a tree. As she sits on the nest, she loses all of her feathers. The male brings her and her chicks all the food they need. When the chicks have all their feathers and the female has grown hers back, the parents open up the hole to let them all out.

NEWLY DISCOVERED CREATURES

The bell pulses in and out to propel the jellyfish forward.

MARIANA TRENCH JELLYFISH
DEEP-SEA NIGHT-LIGHT

For three months in 2016, the *Okeanos Explorer* research vessel explored the Mariana Trench—the deepest place in all the world's oceans. On one dive, they found this beautiful jellyfish more than two miles below the surface. It doesn't have a name yet, but it will soon!

Scientists think that the jellyfish waits with its tentacles outstretched until prey swims by.

HOG-NOSED RAT
PIG-FACED RODENT

In 2013, in a remote area of Indonesia, a team of scientists found a kind of rat that had never been seen before. The new rodent is about the size of a normal rat and is carnivorous, snacking on worms and larvae.

AQUITANIAN PIKE

OVERLOOKED

In 2014, a researcher identified this fish in northern France. The Aquitanian pike looks very similar to other species of pike, so it had gone unnoticed.

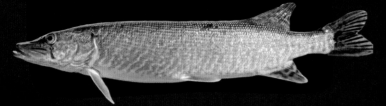

PEACOCK SPIDERS

SPIDER SHOW-OFFS

In 2015, a graduate student in Queensland, Australia, discovered these two new species of peacock spiders. She named one of them Sparklemuffin and the other Skeletorus.

GHOST OCTOPUS

GELATINOUS OCTOPOD

Nearly 2.5 miles below the surface, in the waters off Hawaii, scientists found this octopus in 2016. The deep-sea octopod has no pigment in its skin. It also has very few muscles.

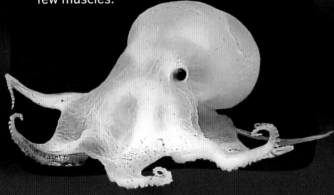

Araguaian River Dolphin

NEWLY FOUND, ALREADY DISAPPEARING

Discovered in the Araguaia River basin in 2014, this freshwater dolphin may already be close to extinction. Of the four previously known species of river dolphins in the world, two are at risk for extinction, and a third may already be gone. No one is sure how many of this species are still around.

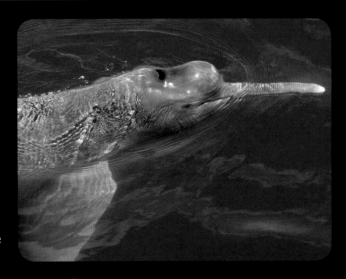

MARKHOR

The markhor is the tallest goat on the planet. It stands nearly 4 feet tall at the shoulder and 6 feet long from nose to tail, and has very long horns that look like giant corkscrews. It lives in the mountains at altitudes of 2,000 to 12,000 feet. The male lives alone and fights with other males over the females during mating season. The female lives in a herd of eight or nine animals with other mothers and their kids. The markhor is an endangered species with many predators, including wolves, leopards, bears, lynx, jackals, and golden eagles. But none are as dangerous as humans, who hunt them for their meat and horns.

The hair is smooth and short in the summer and grows long and thick in the winter.

OKAPI
ANOTHER ELUSIVE ARTIODACTYL

Markhor belong to a group called *artiodactyls*. Animals in this group have four legs and hooves with two or four toes. Another unusual artiodactyl, the okapi, lives in the Democratic Republic of Congo, in central Africa. The okapi is a shy creature. Its dark brown fur and striped legs help it hide in the dappled light of the forest. In fact, the okapi is so good at avoiding humans that it was not described by Europeans until 1901.

That's a big corkscrew!

Twisty horns can be as long as 5 feet in males.

Keen eyesight comes in handy for avoiding predators.

A strong sense of smell allows markhors to detect hidden predators.

A beard under the markhor's chin can grow to 2 feet long.

CREATURE FEATURES

Scientific Name
Capra falconeri

Class
Mammals

Height
Up to 4 feet (1.2 m) tall

Weight
Males: up to 250 pounds (113 kg);
females: up to 110 pounds (50 kg)

Habitat
Steep, rocky mountainsides

Diet
Grass, leaves, herbs, fruit, and flowers

Range
Afghanistan, Pakistan, Kashmir, Tajikistan, and Uzbekistan

Conservation Status
Near Threatened

LEAF ME ALONE!

Hornlike points over its eyes give the Malayan horned frog its name—and help it hide in leaf litter on the rain forest floor.

CHRISTMAS FRIGATEBIRD

Like many birds, male and female Christmas frigatebirds look different. Females are black with a white chest and belly and pink bill. They are larger than the males, which are all black with a small white patch on their bellies and a gray bill. But the male's most distinctive feature is a red pouch under its bill that it puffs up to attract females. *Cool trick!* Frigatebird parents build their nests high in tall trees in the forests of Christmas Island, Australia. Females lay only one egg every other year, and both parents take turns sitting on the nest until their baby is hatched. When not on the nest, frigatebirds can travel hundreds of miles without stopping. While they cannot walk well or swim, they are excellent fliers. One mother was tracked traveling 1,000 miles on an 11-day journey in search of food for her chick. The Christmas frigatebird eats flying fish and sometimes steals food from other seabirds. That is how it got its nickname, "sky pirate."

GREATER PRAIRIE CHICKEN

ANOTHER PUFFER

The greater prairie chicken is a beautiful grouse with brown-and-white-striped feathers. Two tufts of feathers stick up on its head and look like ears. The male has a bright orange air sac on either side of his neck that he inflates to attract females. *Big ears and a puffed-up head. Now, that's attractive!*

Welcome to the island of the sky pirates!

CREATURE FEATURES

Scientific Name
Fregata andrewsi

Class
Birds

Length
About 3 feet (90 cm), with wingspan of up to 8 feet (2.5 m)

Weight
Up to 3.5 pounds (1.6 kg)

Life Span
Up to 45 years

Home
Nests in tall forest trees. When not breeding, the birds range hundreds of miles.

Diet
Flying fish, squid, carrion, and eggs

Range
Indian Ocean and the seas of Southeast Asia. Only breeds on Christmas Island, in the Indian Ocean.

Conservation Status
Critically Endangered

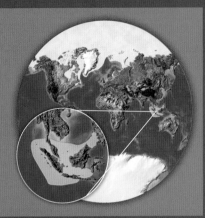

Keen eyesight comes in handy when avoiding predators.

A pink bill and white chest and belly identify this bird as a female.

The long hooked beak snatches fish from the ocean while the bird is still in flight.

This great frigatebird is showing off his throat patch in hopes of attracting a mate.

Long forked tail allows for fast and acrobatic turns in flight.

FABULOUS FEET

 IGUANA

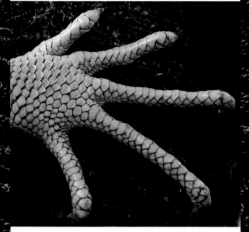

▶ **Trees along rivers in Central and South America**
Five toes with sharp claws grab leaves and bark, making this lizard an excellent climber.

 HORSE

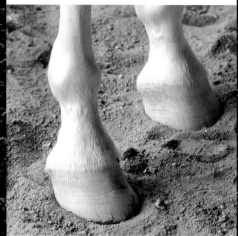

▶ **Domesticated worldwide**
Horse hooves are made of keratin, the same stuff that makes up your hair and nails!

 BLACK BEAR

▶ **Forests in North America**
These claws are used for digging up roots and bulbs, digging dens, climbing, and marking trees.

JAPANESE MACAQUE

▶ **Forests in Japan**
This monkey has back feet that can grasp branches and help it climb.

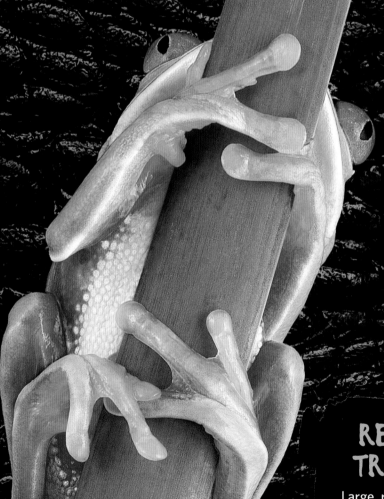

RED-EYED TREE FROG

Large, round toes provide more sticky area to help tree frogs cling to branches and rocks.

CAMEL

 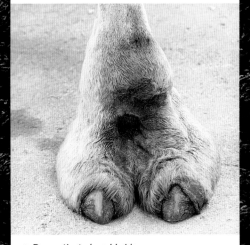

▸ Domesticated worldwide
Its broad toes make a wide base, and pads on the bottom of the feet provide protection.

GALÁPAGOS TORTOISE

▸ Galápagos Islands, Ecuador
Strong legs and claws help the tortoise dig burrows to wait out hot weather.

SITATUNGA

▸ Swamps and marshes in central Africa
The hooves of this marsh-dwelling antelope allow it to walk silently in water.

NILE CROCODILE

▸ Rivers throughout Africa
Strong claws on the front feet dig in to hold ground when capturing prey. The back feet are webbed.

TOKAY GECKO

 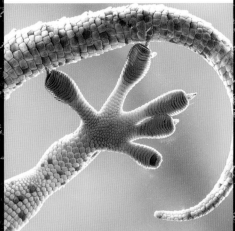

▸ Rain forests in Southeast Asia
Tiny hairs on the bottom of these feet allow them to stick to and unstick from surfaces.

NEW ZEALAND FALCON

▸ New Zealand
Sharp talons hold tight to prey and rip through fur, feathers, and flesh.

BENGAL TIGER

▸ Throughout the Indian subcontinent
The tiger's sharp claws are retractable, disappearing into the paw when not in use.

ASIAN ELEPHANT

 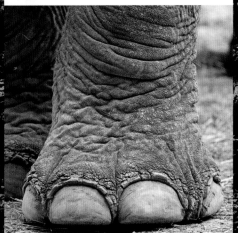

▸ Throughout India and Southeast Asia
Big, padded feet allow this very large animal to move quietly.

MALLARD

▸ Wetlands in North America, Europe, and Asia
Webbed feet distribute this duck's weight when it walks on mud, and help it move in the water.

THORNY DRAGON

The thorny dragon, also known as the thorny devil, looks like it came from prehistoric times. Its camouflaged body is covered in hard, sharp spikes, and it has two large horns on its thorny head. It also has an extra false head growing on its shoulders! When larger animals try to attack it, the thorny dragon dips its real head and shows off the fake one to confuse its attacker. That ploy will only work for a moment, and a bite to the shoulder can still cause a lot of damage, so the thorny dragon is prepared with a backup plan. It can also inflate its chest with air to make itself look bigger. If that's not enough, sharp spines all over its body make it difficult to swallow. *Who would want to eat a thorny, two-headed, puffed-up dragon?* The thorny dragon moves in a mysterious manner. It rocks from side to side as it crawls across the desert, stopping occasionally to strike a perfectly frozen pose.

Mottled color camouflages the lizard in sand and scrub. It can also change color.

Nothing is scarier than a two-headed dragon!

CREATURE FEATURES

Scientific Name
Moloch horridus

Class
Reptiles

Length
Up to 8 inches (20 cm)

Life Span
Up to 20 years

Habitat
Arid scrubland and desert

Home
Burrows into the ground on cold nights to keep warm

Diet
Eats thousands of ants a day

Range
Central and western Australia

Conservation Status
Least Concern

A false head growing on one shoulder distracts predators from their real target.

Ridged scales capture moisture and move it by capillary action to the lizard's mouth.

Sticky tongue catches thousands of ants a day.

Chest can inflate with air to make it look bigger and more intimidating.

Sharp spines all over its body make the lizard difficult to swallow.

PHILIPPINE EAGLE

The Philippine eagle lives in the forests of the Philippines. It is one of the rarest and most powerful birds in the world, with a wingspan of over 7 feet. Its main diet is monkeys and medium-sized mammals, a fact that has earned it a second name, "monkey-eating eagle." It hunts during the day, beginning at the top of a mountain and moving down from tree to tree. This allows it to soar from one location to another, conserving energy since it doesn't have to flap its wings. Two eagles will sometimes hunt together, one soaring overhead to distract a group of monkeys while the other swoops in for the kill. Because of habitat destruction, the Philippine eagle is critically endangered, with fewer than 750 left in the wild. Mating pairs have only one chick every two years, making the population slow to recover.

Luckily, the only known predators of the eagle are humans. The birds have been protected as the national bird of the Philippines since 1995. Killing one is punishable by 12 years in jail!

Wingspan of over 7 feet is short for a bird of its size, allowing it to maneuver among tree branches.

CREATURE FEATURES

Scientific Name
Pithecophaga jefferyi

Class
Birds

Length
Up to 4 feet (1.2 m), with a wingspan of more than 6 feet (2 m)

Weight
Up to 18 pounds (8 kg)

Life Span
Up to 60 years

Habitat
Lowland and mountain rain forests

Nest
Builds an enormous nest, up to 9 feet (2.8 m) in diameter

Diet
Monkeys, snakes, and lizards

Range
Found only in the Philippines

Conservation Status
Critically Endangered

Males and females both have a distinctive shaggy crest.

Keen eyes can spot small prey from the air.

Hooked beak is designed for ripping flesh.

Monkeys for dinner, reptiles for dessert.

VANISHING CREATURES

Common Angelshark

VANISHING WORLDWIDE

This bottom-dweller used to be common, but is now extinct through most of its previous range. The shark can still be found in the Canary Islands, where conservationists are trying to save it.

MADAGASCAR POCHARD

DUCK, DUCK, GONE

This diving duck, which lives only on the island of Madagascar, was declared extinct in 1991. Then, in 2006, a small flock was discovered. There are only about 20 left in the wild, but with a captive breeding program in place, there is still hope for the species.

RED RIVER GIANT SOFTSHELL

SACRED TURTLE

This turtle is the largest in the world. It's also the rarest. Scientists are still hoping to save it through a breeding program, but there are only three left in captivity, and likely none in the wild.

Narrow, curved beak is used for digging insects out of the dirt.

NORTHERN BALD IBIS

BIRD IN PERIL

More than 95% of the remaining bald ibis population is found in Morocco. About 300 of these birds are there.

Leathery shell can be up to 40 inches long, and the turtle can weigh nearly 300 pounds.

HAINAN GIBBON
IN DANGER OF DISAPPEARING

Only about 25 of these monkeys still live in a small preserve on an island off the coast of China. They spend their entire lives in the treetops, eating fruits, leaves, and insects. Scientists keep a close eye on them. Because there are so few left, one large storm or illness could wipe out the whole population.

Pushed out of their natural habitat over time, the last remaining troop is critically endangered.

PLOUGHSHARE TORTOISE
RARE PLANT-EATER

The last of the ploughshare tortoises live on the northwestern coast of Madagascar. There are about 200 left in the wild.

JAVAN RHINOCEROS
POACHED TO THE BRINK

Like all rhinos, the Javan rhino is threatened by poachers. There are probably about 60 left in the rain forests and wetlands of Southeast Asia.

Horn is used to scrape hollows for wallowing.

LION'S MANE JELLYFISH

Despite their name, jellyfish are not fish. They're invertebrates—creatures without backbones. The lion's mane jellyfish is one of the largest jellyfish. Its bell can grow up to 8 feet in diameter and its tentacles can reach over 100 feet. *That's longer than two school buses put together.* The lion's mane jellyfish likes open water where it can ride ocean currents. It loves cold water and is found in the Arctic, the northern Atlantic, and the northern Pacific Oceans. It is most abundant in the English Channel. That was probably how the British mystery writer Sir Arthur Conan Doyle heard about it. The jellyfish became popular when he featured it in a Sherlock Holmes story, "The Adventure of the Lion's Mane." Even though the jellyfish in that story turned out to be the murder weapon, the lion's mane jellyfish is not considered dangerous. Its sting is painful, but rarely fatal.

Thin muscles contract to move the edges of the bell in and out, propelling the jellyfish forward.

A 100-foot surfer!

CREATURE FEATURES

Scientific Name
Cyanea capillata

Class
Sea jellies

Length
Bell usually grows to 20 inches (50 cm), but can grow as large as 8 feet (2.5 m) in diameter.
Tentacles can reach over 100 feet (30 m) in length.

Life Span
Probably less than 1 year

Habitat
Cold open waters

Diet
Fish and other jellyfish, zooplankton when young

Range
Arctic and northern Pacific and Atlantic Oceans

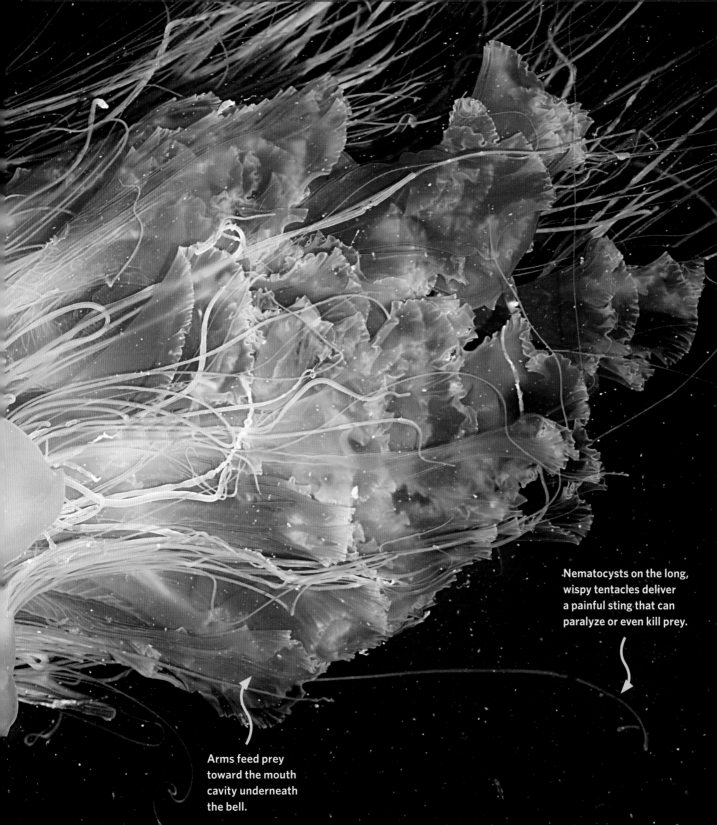

Nematocysts on the long, wispy tentacles deliver a painful sting that can paralyze or even kill prey.

Arms feed prey toward the mouth cavity underneath the bell.

GROSS IS USED INSTEAD OF YUCK
FOR WORDS LIKE POOP AND PUS,
BUT ALL THESE ANIMALS AGREE—
IT'S ONLY GROSS TO US!

BUGGING OUT

 HICKORY HORNED DEVIL

▶ Midwestern, southern, and eastern US
Named for the black-tipped "horns" on its body, this moth caterpillar is completely harmless.

 AFRICAN PAPER WASP

▶ Africa and southwestern Asia
This busy worker chews up wood, which it will mix with saliva to build a paper nest.

 EUROPEAN RHINOCEROS BEETLE

▶ Europe and the Mediterranean basin
An active nighttime flier, the adult rhinoceros beetle does not eat.

 AUSTRALIAN HOUSE CENTIPEDE

▶ Australia
This fast-moving insect hunter is deceptively named—it has only 30 legs.

PUSS MOTH CATERPILLAR

If threatened, this caterpillar will arch its back, raising its red snout and tail. Fail to heed the warning and you might be sprayed with formic acid!

KATYDID

► **Worldwide**
There are more than 6,000 species of katydids spread out across the world.

 ### IO MOTH

► **Central America**
Spots on this moth's wings look like the eyes of a larger animal, discouraging predators.

 ### JAPANESE GIANT HORNET

► **Japan**
Growing to almost 2 inches long, this giant wasp can deliver a painful sting, so steer clear!

 ### LEAF-FOOTED BUG

► **Worldwide**
There are almost 2,000 species of leaf-footed bugs, named for the flat sections on their back legs.

 ### SLUG CATERPILLAR

► **South America**
The hairy spines can deliver a painful sting, but its bright yellow spots warn most away.

 ### MADAGASCAR HISSING COCKROACH

► **Madagascar**
This harmless cockroach is named for the sound it makes blowing air out of special holes in its shell.

 ### THORN TREEHOPPERS

► **South America**
A pointed shell provides camouflage for these insects, which look like the thorns of a plant.

 ### LANTERN BUG

► **Southeast Asia**
Also known as lantern flies, these insects don't actually light up.

 ### WHEEL BUG

► **North America**
Look out—when harassed, this assassin bug can let off a stinky smell.

BOBBIT WORM

The Bobbit worm is the world's longest bristleworm. It lives on the ocean floor and can grow up to 10 feet long. Its segmented body looks like a bright rainbow. It has two pairs of powerful jaws that look like claws and hidden eyes at the base of its five antennae. The Bobbit worm buries its long body in the ocean bed and patiently waits for approaching prey, which it senses with its antennae. It is armed with very sharp teeth and the ability to attack with such speed that it can slice a fish in half. It can grab a fish and disappear with it in less than half a second!

Five antennae sense vibrations and chemical changes in the water that indicate prey is nearby.

Beware of the rainbow!

Two pairs of jaws give a nasty bite.

CREATURE FEATURES

Scientific Name
Eunice aphroditois

Class
Bristleworms

Length
Up to 10 feet (3 m) long

Habitat
Seafloor up to 130 feet (40 m) deep

Home
Buries itself in gravel or sand

Diet
Animals dwelling on or near the seafloor (mostly fish and mollusks)

Range
Indo-Pacific region, possibly in other warm seas

Conservation Status
Not Evaluated

Lobes called *parapodia* are found on each segment of the worm's body. They help the worm move in the water and under the seafloor.

The pharynx turns inside out to capture prey.

When the Bobbit worm's body catches the light, it shimmers, rainbow-colored, like a soap bubble.

CHINESE SOFTSHELL TURTLE

The Chinese softshell turtle spends most of its life underwater, dug safely into the muddy bottoms of lakes and rivers. It has a long neck and pointed snout that it sticks up out of shallow water so it can breathe. The turtle can also absorb oxygen through its skin and throat, which allows it to stay submerged in deeper water for most of the day. It has a pliable shell and webbed feet that it uses for swimming. The female lays up to 30 round eggs at a time in a nest dug about 6 inches into the ground near the water. When the Chinese softshell turtle feels threatened, it releases a stinky smell from its rear end. *A skunk turtle?* But that's not what's gross about this creature. While many animals flush urea from their systems by peeing, the Chinese softshell turtle releases most of the urea in its body by rinsing out its mouth. You might even say it's urinating through its mouth.

Shell does not have the bony scales of hard-shelled turtles. It is leathery and can be bent.

MATA MATA
FELLOW SNORKELER

The mata mata lives in the Amazon and Orinoco basins of South America. It is a large turtle with a horn at the end of its snout, a very long neck, and a flat, triangular head. It wades in shallow water with its snout sticking out and breathes through its horn like a snorkel. *Now, that's cool!*

CREATURE FEATURES

Scientific Name
Pelodiscus sinensis

Class
Reptiles

Length
Grows to 1 foot (30 cm)

Life Span
Up to 6 years

Habitat
Rivers, ponds, and creeks

Home
Spends most of the day buried in mud at the bottoms of rivers and ponds

Diet
Small fish, crustaceans, and insects

Range
China, Taiwan, northern Vietnam, North and South Korea, Japan, and Russia

Conservation Status
Vulnerable

Long snout can stick up while the turtle remains hidden in the water.

Now, THAT'S gross!

Its strong jaws make short work of crustacean and mollusk shells.

Long neck can stretch to capture food, and be drawn back into the shell if the turtle is threatened.

The Chinese softshell turtle is an excellent swimmer. Webbed feet allow it to maneuver in the water.

POOP!

KOALA
WORLD'S GROSSEST BABY FOOD

When a baby koala is weaning from its mother's milk, it first eats pap, a modified form of feces produced by its mother. The pap contains beneficial bacteria that the baby will need to start digesting tough eucalyptus leaves.

DUNG BEETLE
DINNER ON A ROLL

The dung beetle rolls other animals' poop into one giant ball of food that contains all the nutrients it needs. The ball will also feed the beetle's young when they hatch from eggs laid—where else?—in poop!

COTTONTAIL RABBIT
TWO-TIMER

Digesting the tough fibers in grass and other plants requires some extra work. Rabbits solve the problem by eating their own poop. The food is partially digested the first time around. On its second trip through the digestive tract, it's ready to break down into usable nutrients.

Parrotfish

POOPERS IN PARADISE

If you've ever visited a beautiful sandy beach near a coral reef, you may have been walking on poop. Parrotfish eat coral rock while grazing on algae on the reef. It comes out the other end as sand. One stoplight parrotfish can make up to 220 pounds of sand a year. A study in the Maldives found that up to 85% of sand in the area was once parrotfish poop.

EARTHWORM

USEFUL POOP

We'd be in a lot of trouble without these wiggly worms. Earthworms swallow plant matter and other debris as they tunnel through dirt. When it comes out the other end, it has been broken down into nutrients that can be used by plants.

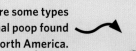

These are some types of animal poop found in North America.

SCAT
IT'S ALL RELATIVE

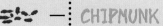 — MOUSE

 — RAT

 — CHIPMUNK

— SQUIRREL

— RABBIT

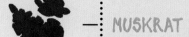 — FISHER

 — MUSKRAT

— RACCOON

— WILD TURKEY

— CANADA GOOSE

 — FOX

 — BLACK BEAR

 — MOOSE

JUMPING SPIDER

LOOK OUT!

Like many spiders, this Asian jumping spider has eight eyes. The two in the front focus in on prey. The eyes on the sides of its head make it possible for the spider to see in all directions.

The hoatzin is a large stinkbird. It has a long neck and a small head . . . and a very foul odor. *A "fowl" odor?* The hoatzin eats leaves and flowers. It ferments its lunch in its digestive system, much like a cow does, which creates a nasty smell. Because of its oversized digestive system, the hoatzin is an awkward bird. Its wing muscles are weak, it can fly only in short bursts, and it is a slow and awkward climber. On top of that, it is loud and likes to groan, croak, hiss, and grunt. The hoatzin lives in colonies of up to 30 noisy, stinky family members, and nests in trees hanging over the water.

A bird that smells like cow manure? EWWW!

Wings and tail provide balance while the bird climbs and perches. It is a poor flier.

ANCIENT BABIES

Hoatzin chicks have claws on their wings, exactly where the claws would have been on the prehistoric archeopteryx. If they are threatened in the nest, the chicks can jump out and use the river for escape. They are then able to climb back to the nest using the claws on their wings and feet. The claws drop off when the chicks are about three months old.

Sharp, strong beak strips leaves from trees.

An organ called the crop holds helpful bacteria that ferments tough plant matter so that it can be digested.

A large, rubbery callus acts as a prop to hold the bird up when it has eaten too much.

CREATURE FEATURES

Scientific Name
Opisthocomus hoazin

Class
Birds

Length
Nearly 30 inches (75 cm)

Weight
Up to 2 pounds (1 kg)

Habitat
Swamps, mangrove forests, and rain forests along rivers and streams

Home
Stick nests in trees overhanging water

Diet
Leaves, flowers, and fruit

Range
Northern South America

Conservation Status
Least Concern

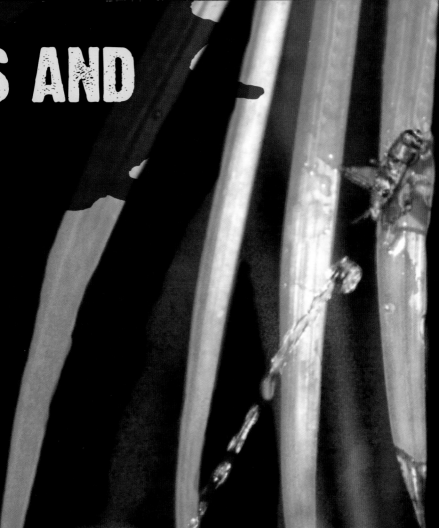

A stream of blood squirts from broken veins around the eye.

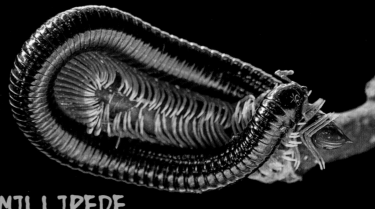

MILLIPEDE
MANY-FOOTED STINK MONSTER

When harassed, a millipede will coil into a tight circle. Many can also secrete a yucky liquid from tiny holes in their shells. In some species, that liquid can burn through the exoskeletons of other bugs.

Horned Lizard
BLOOD-SQUIRTING EYES

This desert-dwelling lizard would prefer to be left alone. If it cannot get away from a predator, it squirts a stream of blood from one eye, startling the attacker and buying time for its escape.

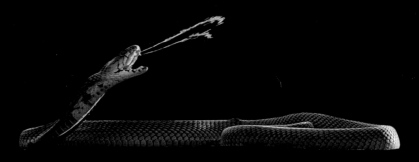

MOZAMBIQUE SPITTING COBRA
CHAMPION SPITTER

While most snakes must bite, this deadly cobra is able to squirt its venom up to 8 feet. Even so, it will often play dead rather than pick a fight.

BIGFIN REEF SQUID
INKY ESCAPE ARTIST

Like many of its fellow cephalopods, this squid can use ink in self-defense. When predators get too close, the squid

OLM

The olm is a European salamander that spends its entire life underwater in a cave. It eats, sleeps, and breeds in complete darkness. Not surprisingly, the olm is mostly blind. Its eyes are covered by a layer of skin, but they can detect differences in light. But its senses of smell, taste, and hearing are exceptional. The olm swims like an eel, twisting its snakelike body and getting an extra boost from its tail, which is short and flat and surrounded by a thin fin. The female lays up to 70 eggs at a time, placing them between rocks to protect them. The olm swallows its prey—insects, snails, and small crabs—whole. It can consume large amounts of food at once and survive for up to 10 years without eating. *It takes fasting to a whole new level!*

Underwater cave critter.

Hind feet have only two toes—three fewer than most salamanders.

Tail is surrounded by a thin fin to propel the olm through the water.

CREATURE FEATURES

Scientific Name
Proteus anguinus

Class
Amphibians

Length
Up to 16 inches (40 cm)

Life Span
More than 100 years

Habitat
Underwater caves in lakes and rivers

Diet
Insect, snails, and small crabs

Range
Southern Europe throughout Slovenia, Bosnia, Herzegovina, and Croatia

Conservation Status
Vulnerable

SAGALLA CAECILIAN
FELLOW SIGHTLESS AMPHIBIAN

Like the olm, the Sagalla caecilian is completely blind. The legless amphibian uses its bony skull to burrow through soil, and a layer of bone and skin covers its eyes. It has a large mouth and three rows of teeth. *They must need a lot of toothpaste!* The Sagalla caecilian is only found on the isolated Sagalla Hill in southeast Kenya.

Covered by skin, the eyes can only sense changes in light.

Its forefeet have three toes—one fewer than most salamanders.

External gills absorb oxygen from the water.

THE THROW-UP THROW-DOWN

HONEYBEES
YOU MIGHT NOT WANT TO READ THIS

Bees make honey by swallowing nectar and storing it in a special stomach full of enzymes. The enzymes break down the nectar, but it's not honey yet. When the bee returns to the hive, it regurgitates the nectar into another bee's mouth, who regurgitates it into another bee's mouth, and so on down the line, until it is ready to be stored as honey.

CATS VS. DOGS
SPOILER ALERT: THEY BOTH BARF

When something that enters the stomach is completely indigestible, odds are good that it will come back up. Cats swallow fur as they groom—when too much of it builds up in the stomach, it comes back as a hairball. No one is sure why dogs eat grass, but grass is frequently found in dog vomit.

CATTLE
CHEW IT ONCE, CHEW IT TWICE

Grass is made of tough cellulose, making it difficult to be chewed and digested. Cows solve this problem by chewing, and digesting, it more than once. After a mouthful makes its way to the cow's stomach, the cow regurgitates it for more chewing before it is sent to the next chamber of the stomach.

Northern Fulmar
THIS BABY WILL MESS YOU UP

Many nestlings are defenseless, but this seabird has an unusual way of staying safe. If a predator approaches the nest, the fulmar chick will regurgitate an oily liquid onto it. The substance is difficult to wash off and is so slimy that it can prevent the attacker from flying or swimming.

GENTOO PENGUIN
BENEVOLENT BARFING

Like many birds, penguins feed their young regurgitated food. The parents travel to the sea and swallow fish. When they return, they regurgitate a meal right from their stomachs into the baby's mouth.

OWLS
BONY BARF

Along with good food, owls gulp a lot of indigestible bones, fur, and teeth. These inedible parts collect in pellets that can be regurgitated.

FLESH FLY
REGURGITATES *BEFORE* EATING

Flies don't have teeth, which makes it difficult for them to eat solids. Flesh flies solve that problem by predigesting their meal. They regurgitate a bubble of digestive enzymes onto their food, letting the juices break the food down into a slurpable ooze.

ANTARCTIC ISOPOD

The Antarctic giant isopod looks like an enormous underwater pill bug. But it is not a bug! It is a marine crustacean similar to a giant crab. It lives at the bottom of the ocean at depths of up to 2,300 feet. The female devotes an unusual amount of energy to her young, carrying hundreds of eggs in a brood pouch that can be as big as her entire body. One Antarctic giant isopod was found with more than 1,000 eggs in her pouch! After incubating for nearly 600 days, the babies emerge as fully mature miniature adults. *That's one dedicated mother!*

A thick exoskeleton protects against predators. If threatened, the isopod will roll into a ball.

Looks like a doodle bug, dines on dead whales.

Two pairs of antennae help the isopod find its way on the dark seafloor.

Each compound eye has nearly 4,000 facets and reflective membranes that help it see in dim light.

Seven pairs of legs are used for crawling and digging into soft sand and mud.

CREATURE FEATURES

Scientific Name
Glyptonotus antarcticus

Super Class
Crustaceans

Length
Up to 5 inches (12 cm)

Weight
Up to 2.5 ounces (70 g)

Habitat
Ocean floor at depths of up to 2,300 feet (700 m)

Home
Burrows into the mud of the ocean floor

Diet
Animal carcasses, plant debris, echinoderms, and other invertebrates

Range
Cold, dark waters of the Antarctic

Conservation Status
Least Concern

SOLDIER FLY

EYE SEE YOU

Each of this fly's eyes is made up
of thousands of *ommatidia*,
tiny facets that allow the fly
to see 360 degrees around it.
You'll have a hard time sneaking
up on this soldier.

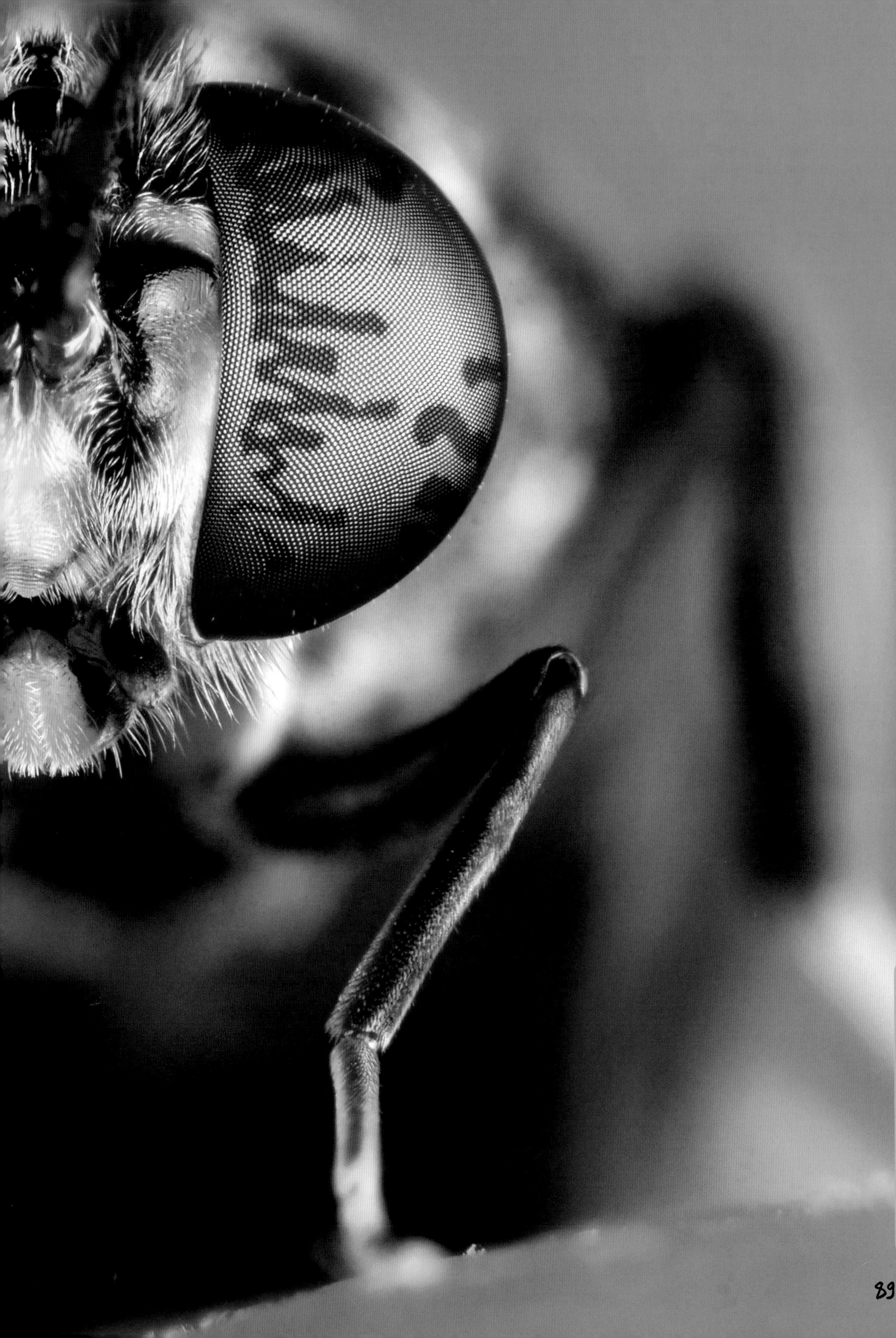

GOLIATH BIRD-EATING SPIDER

The Goliath bird-eating spider got its name from an 18th-century engraving by naturalist Maria Sibylla Merian that shows the spider eating a hummingbird. Truth is, the Goliath bird-eating spider rarely ever preys on birds. *It's too busy chasing toads!* The Goliath bird-eating spider is the most massive spider in the world. Fortunately, it is secretive and will quickly retreat into its burrow when larger animals approach. When it is threatened, it makes a loud hissing sound by rubbing the bristles on its legs. The hissing can be heard up to 15 feet away. It also rears up, flings its barbed abdominal hairs, and bites with its 1.5-inch fangs when stressed. It spends most of its time in an underground burrow. The female produces up to 200 eggs, which she stores in a silk pouch about 1 inch across. If she ever has to leave home, she takes the egg pouch with her.

GOLIATH BEETLE
FELLOW RAIN FOREST GIANT

The Goliath beetle is one of the largest insects on Earth. It can grow up to 5 inches long. The Goliath beetle lives in the rain forests of Africa, where it feeds on fruit, dung, tree sap, plant matter, and the remains of dead animals. Like the Goliath bird-eating spider, this oversized insect was named after the biblical character Goliath, a giant who was slain by tiny David with a slingshot.

The most massive spider in the world.

Broader hairs toward the end of the legs stick to surfaces when climbing.

Bristly hairs, called *setae*, can be rubbed together to make sound.

CREATURE FEATURES

Scientific Name
Theraphosa blondi

Class
Arachnids

Length
Up to 5 inches (12.7 cm), with leg span up to 1 foot (30 cm)

Weight
Up to 6 ounces (175 g)

Life Span
Females: up to 20 years; males: up to 6 years

Habitat
Rain forests

Home
A silk-lined burrow in the ground

Diet
Insects, earthworms, and small vertebrates

Range
Northern South America

Conservation Status
Not Evaluated

BLOBBY, SLIMY, STRETCHY CREATURES

Eyestalks can be pulled into the body for protection.

SLUG

SHELL-LESS MOLLUSK

The slug is made up of mostly water and is most active after a rain. When it is threatened, it contracts its body into a round, compact shape.

OCTOPUS

NO BONES ABOUT IT

The octopus has two eyes and four pairs of arms, but no internal or external skeleton. It can escape from large predators by squeezing itself through tight places. This one made a home out of someone else's trash.

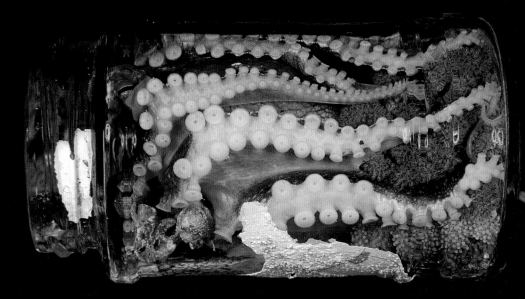

Slime Mold

NOT EXACTLY AN ANIMAL

Once believed to be fungi, this colony of amoebas can change shape and move as a single body. It is most commonly found in forests.

NUDIBRANCH

COLORFUL MOLLUSK

Its other name is sea slug. It can swallow the stinging cells from a jellyfish and transfer them to its own skin, stealing its victim's defenses.

LEECH

VAMPIRE WORM

Leeches live both in water and on land. They are known for sucking blood, but plenty are carnivores or scavengers. Leeches have suckers at both ends of their bodies that allow them to attach to objects and food sources.

SEA CUCUMBER

OCEAN-DWELLER

Not a vegetable at all, this sluglike animal lives on the ocean floor and is related to sea stars. It can discharge a sticky thread to ensnare its enemies. It breathes through its anus, and it does not have a brain.

COOL IS HOW WE THINK WE LOOK
WHEN WE TRY TO IMPRESS,
BUT ANIMALS ARE BORN THAT WAY—
WITH LOTS OF COOL FINESSE!

CHANGEABLE LIZARD

BRIGHT FUTURE

This young changeable lizard might not be brown for long. When they're adults, male changeable lizards have red heads during mating season. They are brown or gray the rest of the year.

BLUE-FOOTED BOOBY

The blue-footed booby is a large seabird with big bright blue feet. The male booby is very proud of its feet and likes to lift them up and down while strutting in front of the female. *Show-off!* The brightness of the male's feet shows how healthy and well fed he is. If the booby hasn't eaten in a while, his feet will be a duller blue. But these cool kicks aren't just for show. Boobies also use their large, webbed feet to cover their chicks and keep them warm in the nest. Because it looks clumsy while walking, the blue-footed booby gets its name from the Spanish word *bobo*, which means "foolish." Silly though it may seem on land, this bird is a graceful diver. From the sky, the booby looks for schools of fish or squid. When it spots its prey, it tucks its wings and plunges into the water, grabbing a well-earned meal.

Coolest kicks of any creature!

CREATURE FEATURES

Scientific Name
Sula nebouxii

Class
Birds

Length
Up to 3 feet (90 cm), with wingspan of nearly 5 feet (1.5 m)

Weight
Up to 4 pounds (2 kg)

Habitat
Rocky shores on Pacific islands

Nest
Digs a steep-sided nest in the sand to lay its eggs

Diet
Fish, flying fish, and squid

Range
Islands in the Pacific Ocean from the Gulf of California to the western coasts of Central and South America

Conservation Status
Least Concern

Nostrils are permanently closed, preventing them from getting waterlogged during dives. The bird breathes from the corner of its bill.

Long bill pierces the water and snags prey.

Wings can be tucked close into the body to dive from as high as 80 feet.

Bright blue feet are webbed for swimming. They also make handy egg warmers.

RED-FOOTED BOOBY
FELLOW FANCY-FOOT

In all, there are seven species of booby. The red-footed booby is the smallest. It looks an awful lot like its blue-footed cousin, with one big difference. *I don't have to tell you what that is!*

VENOMOUS CREATURES

KING COBRA
DEADLY CHARMER

This is one of the world's most deadly snakes. It produces large amounts of venom and can kill an elephant with just one bite.

PUSS CATERPILLAR
PAINFUL PET

This caterpillar may look like a furry little pet, but don't pet it! Its soft-looking fur hides venomous bristles underneath. Its venom causes intense throbbing pain, and may even cause some people to lose consciousness. As a moth, it's harmless.

Suckers on each tentacle grasp prey and help pull the octopus along on solid surfaces.

BLUE-RINGED OCTOPUS
NICKNAMED "BRO"

It is small enough to fit in the palm of your hand, but only 1 milligram of venom from this deadly BRO can kill. There is no known antidote.

Brazilian Wandering Spider

WEB-LESS ARACHNID

The wandering spider is one of the most venomous spiders on the planet. It does not build a web. It wanders the forest at night, hunting for prey such as insects, other spiders, small reptiles, amphibians, and mice.

SEA WASP

MOST DEADLY JELLYFISH

The tentacles of this very dangerous jellyfish can be up to 10 feet long and contain millions of nematocysts. Although the venom in those stinging cells is fast-acting and potent, swimmers who are stung and make it to shore can be treated with antivenom, and most survive.

STONEFISH

LOOKS LIKE A ROCK

The most venomous fish in the world lives near underwater rocks and coral reefs and buries itself in the sand in shallow waters. It grows up to 20 inches and weighs up to 5 pounds.

MWANZA FLAT-HEADED ROCK AGAMA

The Mwanza flat-headed rock agama looks like Spider-Man and can climb walls just like him, too! The male's head, neck, and shoulders are bright red, and its body is dark blue. The bright colors help attract mates and identify the male as dominant. But being bright blue and red has its drawbacks when you live in the semi-desert, so the male can change his color to brown at night or when he is frightened. He also develops white spots on his body when he gets into a fight with another male. The rock agama spends its days sunbathing on warm rocks and snacking on locusts, crickets, and worms. *The perfect diet for a superhero.*

Puts on a superhero suit to attract attention!

Males change their colors to brown at night or when they're threatened. Females are always brown.

The tail is used like a whip in fights with other agamas.

CREATURE FEATURES

Scientific Name
Agama mwanzae

Class
Reptiles

Length
Up to 1 foot (30 cm)

Life Span
Up to 15 years

Habitat
Rock outcrops in high savanna and grassland

Home
Shelters under and in the spaces between large boulders; sometimes found in crevices around homes as well

Diet
Locusts, crickets, and worms, occasionally seeds and berries

Range
Tanzania, Rwanda, and Kenya, in east Africa

Conservation Status
Least Concern

Small scales protect the skin and prevent water loss.

Tiny front teeth chew up prey before it is swallowed.

WOLF'S MONA MONKEY

FELLOW SUPERHERO IMPERSONATOR

The Wolf's mona monkey forages for fruit and insects in the rain forests of central Africa. Colorful examples of this species look an awful lot like the X-Men's Wolverine. Luckily, they're far more peaceful than the aggressive superhero.

Sharp claws grab small bumps in rocks for quick running and climbing.

103

LONG-TAILED PANGOLIN

The long-tailed pangolin looks like a cross between a pinecone and an armadillo. It lives in trees and dines on ants and termites. When it finds them, it tears their nests apart with its sharp claws and slurps the insects with its long, sticky tongue. It is estimated that a pangolin can eat 70 million ants and termites in a year. The long-tailed pangolin has a most remarkable tail. Longer than its entire body, the tail is strong enough to hold the pangolin's whole weight as it dangles from branches. Baby pangolins also ride on their mother's tails until they are weaned. When threatened, the long-tailed pangolin curls up into a ball and makes sharp movements with its scales. It also emits a disgusting secretion from its anal glands, like a skunk does. *Pee-yew! Looks like a pinecone and smells like a skunk!*

Prickly pest control.

Its eyes are protected from insect attacks by thick eyelids. It can also close its ears and nostrils.

Its strong sense of smell leads the pangolin to ant nests in the trees.

A sticky tongue, up to 10 inches (25.4 cm) long, slurps ants and termites from their nests.

No teeth. The pangolin swallows its tiny prey whole.

Its large foreclaws pull apart insect nests.

Hornlike, overlapping scales are made of keratin, the same material that is in human fingernails!

Prehensile tail is strong enough to hold the pangolin's entire weight.

CREATURE FEATURES

Scientific Name
Phataginus tetradactyla

Class
Mammals

Length
3.7 to 4.5 inches (95 to 115 cm)

Weight
4.5 to 5.5 pounds (2 to 2.5 kg)

Habitat
Forests near rivers and swamps with palm and specialized swamp trees

Home
Spends most of its life in trees; likes to sleep in tree hollows or hollowed-out insect nests

Diet
Ants and termites

Range
West and Central Africa

Conservation Status
Vulnerable

105

THE EYES HAVE IT

 CHAMELEON

▶ Rain forests of Africa and Madagascar
This lizard can keep an eye on one object while swiveling the other to check out something new.

 CUTTLEFISH

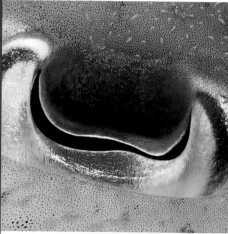

▶ Indian Ocean
The cuttlefish cannot see color, but it can detect the polarization of light.

 HARRIER

▶ Open areas across Europe and Asia
Like all birds of prey, the harrier has keen eyesight to help it spot small animals from the air.

 TREE FROG

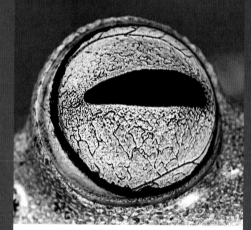

▶ Worldwide
Frog pupils come in different shapes, including stars and triangles. This one is a horizontal slit.

DAMSELFLY
Compound eyes and a broad head give this dragonfly-like insect a wide field of vision.

PHILIPPINES CROCODILE

▶ **Rivers and marshes in the Philippines**
When the crocodile attacks, a transparent eyelid covers and protects its eyes.

 CHINESE WATER DRAGON

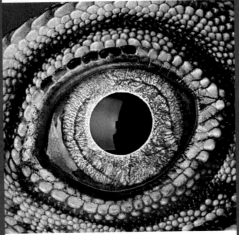

▶ **Forests of China and Southeast Asia**
These reptiles have a light-sensing gland, sometimes called a third eye, between their two normal eyes.

 GIANT PACIFIC OCTOPUS

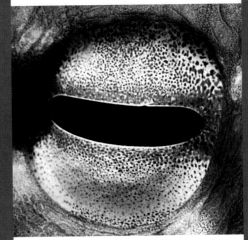

▶ **Waters of the northern Pacific Ocean**
Vision is important to the octopus. Its eyes are similar to a human's.

 DOMESTIC CAT

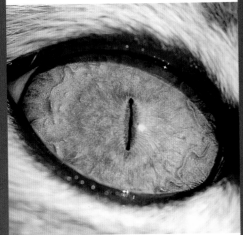

▶ **Worldwide**
Light bounces off a reflective layer in the cat's eye, making it easier for the cat to see in the dark.

 HORNBILL

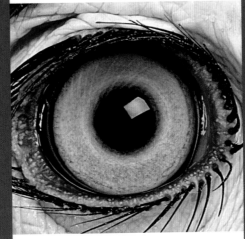

▶ **Forests in Southeast Asia**
Thick "eyelashes" of modified feathers help shield this bird's eyes from sunlight.

 PARROTFISH

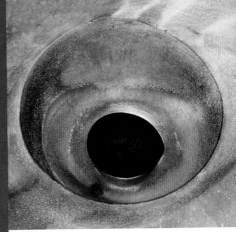

▶ **Coral reefs in the Caribbean Sea**
The colors on this fish's eye continue its body pattern, making the fish harder to spot—and catch!

 DOMESTIC GOAT

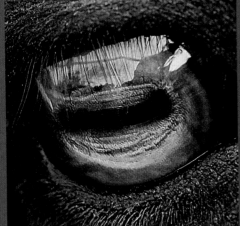

▶ **Worldwide**
Horizontal pupils help grazers such as goats watch for danger while eating.

 LEOPARD GECKO

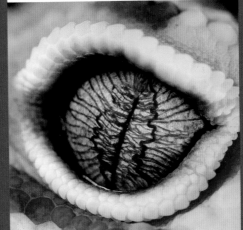

▶ **Forests of the Indian subcontinent**
Vertical pupils are common in ambush predators, which wait for prey to come close and then pounce.

 OWL BUTTERFLY

▶ **Forests of Central and South America**
This clever fake is an eyespot on a butterfly's wing—designed to keep birds from eating it.

GLASS FROG

The glass frog is tiny with soft lime-green skin and large, forward-facing eyes. It has translucent skin on its belly that allows you to see its liver, heart, and intestines without an X-ray machine, just like Superman can! It lives high in treetops and goes down to the ground during mating season. The glass frog is nocturnal and eats insects and spiders. The male is territorial and will let out a low warning sound when another male approaches. If the other male does not back off, it will jump on the intruder's back and chase it away. The female lays up to 35 eggs on the underside of a leaf that hangs above water. The male protects the eggs from insects and parasites until the tadpoles are hatched. The glass frog has many predators, including snakes, mammals, and birds. If it manages to avoid them, it can live up to 14 years.

The heart and other internal organs can be seen through the skin.

Brown spots on the irises break them up visually and help the frog hide against a leafy background.

No X-ray required!

See-through eggs are laid on the underside of leaves overhanging water. When the tadpoles hatch, they fall into the water.

CREATURE FEATURES

Scientific Name
Hayalinobatrachium aureoguttatum

Class
Amphibians

Length
Up to 1 inch (2.5 cm)

Life Span
Up to 14 years

Habitat
Rain forests

Home
Lives high in treetops, coming down to the ground during mating season

Diet
Insects and spiders

Range
Panama, Ecuador, and Colombia

Conservation Status
Near Threatened

SEE-THROUGH CREATURES

LEAFHOPPER NYMPH

AMAZING MOVER

It moves quickly in every direction: forward, backward, and sideways. In its adult phase, it will be an opaque leafhopper, and suck the sap from plants.

The wings do not have colored scales in their centers.

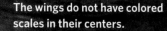

Glasswing Butterfly

UNUSUAL DIET

This delicate see-through creature sips the nectar of sweet flowers—and dines on bird droppings! It lives in Central and South America.

PELAGIC OCTOPUS

CLEAR AS A BELL

It is one of the most transparent of all the animals, with only its eyes and intestinal tract visible.

SEA GOOSEBERRY

BODY OF WATER

Its transparent body is composed of 99% water! When it refracts light, it produces a cascade of rainbow colors.

TORTOISE BEETLE
TRANSPARENT ARMOR

This insect's outer shell may be see-through, but it still provides protection from predators.

CAVE CRAYFISH
CHANGES ITS SHELL

This crustacean molts as it grows, discarding its old shell for a new, larger one. It has a life span of up to 50 years and spends its entire life in underground water systems.

PIGLET SQUID
SURFACE SWIMMER

It has paddle-like fins at the end of its pig-shaped body and swims near the surface of the ocean.

SEA ANGEL
WATER WINGS

It uses its "wings" to swim and looks like a tiny angel flying through the sea. In reality, it is far from heavenly. These sea slugs spend their days hunting their cousins, sea butterflies.

BIG SKATE
PLAYS PEEKABOO

It grows up to nearly 8 feet long and lives in the ocean at depths of up to 2,600 feet. It buries itself in the ocean floor and hides with only its eyes showing.

BOXER MANTIS

PUT UP YOUR DUKES!

When it encounters other mantises, this insect waves its forelegs in slow circles to show off the markings on the insides of its front legs.

GLOW-IN-THE-DARK CREATURES

Tiny hairs, called cilia, refract light.

DINOFLAGELLATE

COLORFUL OCEAN LIGHTS

This colorful, luminescent, ocean-dwelling creature is a single-celled organism. Its glow can be seen in the wake of ships passing at night.

COMB JELLY

OCEAN FLASHLIGHT

Comb jellies move using tiny hairs, called *cilia*. The cilia refract light from outside sources, making the jelly appear to shine, but it is not actually producing its own light.

Firefly

BRIGHT BEETLE

Fireflies are beetles that can produce light of various colors. They can synchronize their flashing lights with other fireflies. They live on every continent except Antarctica.

LANTERN FISH
UNDERWATER GLOW STICK

It lives deep in the ocean at depths of up to 3,000 feet. Its light is created by the same chemical reaction that occurs inside a green glow stick.

GLOWWORM
IT'S NOT A WORM

It resembles a worm, but it's a beetle! Specifically, it's a beetle larva. In railroad worms the larvae and adult female glow. While the adult male resembles other beetles, the adult female never grows wings.

BOBTAIL SQUID
TINY GLOWER

It's only as big as your thumb and hides in the sand during the day. One of its best tricks is that it can control its glow to match the moonlight!

CLUSTERWINK SNAIL
FLASHING SHELL

This tiny snail uses its shell like a lampshade, diffusing its light, which flashes like a blue-green lightbulb. It lives in low-tide areas off the eastern Australian coast.

DEEP-SEA ANGLERFISH
LIGHT LURE

It wears a light at the end of its "fishing pole" to attract its prey. It lives in the dark depths of the ocean, up to a mile below the surface, and can grow up to 3 feet long.

DUCK-BILLED PLATYPUS

The duck-billed platypus is the strangest creature you'll ever meet. It has a bill like a duck, a tail like a beaver, and feet like an otter; it lays eggs like a chicken and walks like a reptile. And it has no teeth! The duck-billed platypus is one of only a handful of mammals that can hunt by detecting the electrical signals created by nerves on the muscles of its prey. It moves its head from side to side while hunting for shrimp, crayfish, worms, and insect larvae. It spends 12 hours a day looking for food, which it gobbles up even though it doesn't have any teeth. Don't think the platypus is defenseless, though. It has a spur on its hind foot that contains venom—a useful defense against predators.

Thick brown fur is waterproof.

Nearly 40,000 electroreceptors receive signals from prey, allowing the platypus to hunt in murky water.

CREATURE FEATURES

Scientific Name
Ornithorhynchus anatinus

Class
Mammals

Length
Up to 2 feet (60 cm)

Weight
Up to 4.5 pounds (2 kg)

Life Span
Up to 20 years

Habitat
Streams, freshwater lakes, and ponds

Home
Digs a burrow in the bank of a stream or pond

Diet
Shrimp, crayfish, worms, insect larvae

Range
Eastern Australia and Tasmania

Conservation Status
Least Concern

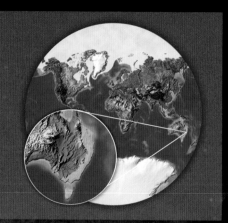

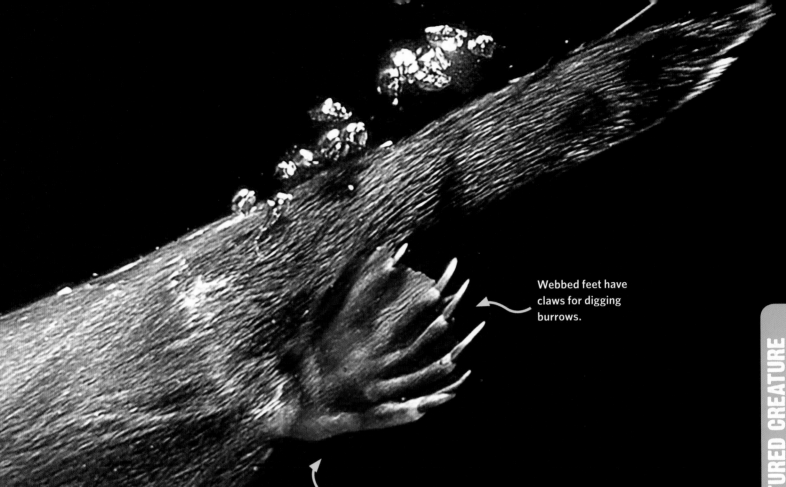

Webbed feet have claws for digging burrows.

Spurs on its back legs contain venom for self-defense.

If it has a bill like a duck and lays eggs like a duck . . . it's STILL not a duck.

WESTERN LONG-BEAKED ECHIDNA
ELECTRIC HUNTER

Electroreception works best underwater, since air is not a good conductor of electricity. Like the platypus, the western long-beaked echidna has electroreceptors in its snout. Although it hunts on land, it uses its snout to root around under leaves, where the damp environment helps conduct the electrical signals of worms.

FANTASTIC FROGS

 SPLENDID LEAF FROG

▶ **Forests in Central America**
As this young leaf frog grows, it will develop the dark green coloring of an adult.

 DYEING POISON FROG

▶ **Rain forests in northeastern South America**
The bright blue color of this ground-dweller warns predators to stay away—it's poisonous.

 BUDGETT'S FROG

▶ **Streams and ponds in central South America**
Don't let this frog's blobby appearance fool you. It has very sharp teeth and is known to bite!

 BLACK-EYED LITTER FROG

▶ **Swampy rain forests in Southeast Asia**
Mottled brown skin allows this cute little creature to hide in the leaf litter of its forest home.

CHACHI TREE FROG

Like all tree frogs, the last bone on each of this frog's toes is curved like a claw, perfect for grabbing stems while climbing.

PIED WARTY FROG

▶ **Tropical forests in Southeast Asia**
It may not surprise you to learn that this tiny brown-and-black frog is often called the bird poop frog.

AMAZON MILK FROG

▶ **Rain forests in northern South America**
When frightened, this canopy-dweller produces a milky, poisonous substance from glands on its back.

PACIFIC HORNED FROG

▶ **Scrub and deserts in Ecuador and Peru**
This rare frog survives dry periods by burrowing underground.

RED-EYED TREE FROG

▶ **Forests in Central America**
Sticky pads on its feet help this climber hold on to leaves and branches as it moves through the trees.

TOMATO FROG

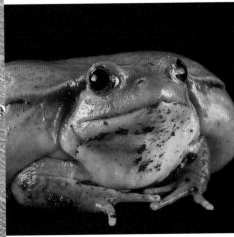

▶ **Rain forests in Madagascar**
Named for its bright red color, it puffs up its body when threatened.

CROSS FROG EGGS

▶ **Rain forests in eastern Papua New Guinea**
Unlike most frogs, these babies of a newly discovered species will hatch from the egg fully formed.

WHITE'S TREE FROG

▶ **Forests in northern and eastern Australia**
This adaptable creature secretes a waxy covering that holds in moisture during dry periods.

WALLACE'S FLYING FROG

▶ **Evergreen rain forests in Indonesia and Malaysia**
Thick webbing between its toes allows this climber to glide up to 50 feet to escape predators.

PAINTED BURROWING FROG

▶ **Rocky canyons in central Madagascar**
This endangered frog has claws for climbing vertical cliffs and bumpy back feet for digging burrows.

CREATURE COLLECTION

119

SWORD-BILLED HUMMINGBIRD

The sword-billed hummingbird is a beautiful bird with shimmering green feathers that look like they are sprinkled with glitter. It is the only bird in the world whose beak is longer than its body. Its bill is so large and heavy that the bird must hold it up high to balance on a perch. The sword-billed hummingbird uses its long bill and long tongue to reach deep into flowers for nectar. Because the bill is too long for preening, the sword-billed hummingbird grooms itself with its feet. *It takes a footbath!* The sword-billed hummingbird lives 10,000 feet up in the mountains. *That's one high flier!*

Wings are connected to the body with an especially flexible joint, allowing the bird to hover in place .

Its feet are larger than other hummingbirds'—perfect for grooming and balancing a heavy beak.

Bill is as long as, or longer than, the bird's body and curves up slightly.

A forked tongue uncurls inside the flower, then curls up to trap nectar and draw it into the bill.

High-flying swordplay.

CREATURE FEATURES

Scientific Name
Ensifera ensifera

Class
Birds

Length
Up to 10 inches (25 cm)

Weight
Up to 0.5 ounce (15 g)

Habitat
Evergreen forests in the mountains, usually at elevations higher than 7,000 feet (2.1 km)

Nest
Builds a cup-shaped nest of plant down

Diet
Nectar

Range
Northwestern South America, from Venezuela and Colombia in the North to Bolivia in the South

Conservation Status
Least Concern

GLOSSARY

Amphibian an animal with a backbone that can live on land and in water

Bioluminescence light created naturally by chemical processes in an animal or plant

Bird a warm-blooded animal that lays eggs, has wings, and is covered in feathers

Breeding producing offspring or young

Burrow a sheltering place dug into the ground

Camouflage a pattern, color, or behavior that helps an animal hide by making it difficult to see

Carrion dead animals or their flesh

Cephalopod a class of invertebrates, such as squid, octopus, and cuttlefish, that have tentacles attached to the head

Class a large grouping of animals that share key traits in common. Animals may be in the same class because they are similar in some large ways, but be in a different genus or species if they do not have enough traits in common to fit into those more specific groupings.

Conservation Status a label given by a conservation group to explain how likely a species is to die off. In this book, the conservation status is taken from the International Union for Conservation of Nature (IUCN). The IUCN has nine categories, five of which are used in the featured creature pages*.

Least Concern the animal has been evaluated and does not qualify as vulnerable or endangered

Vulnerable at high risk of becoming extinct in the wild

Endangered at extremely high risk of becoming extinct in the wild because it meets many criteria, including a population that is getting smaller, habitat that is disappearing or being broken up by human development, or a very small range.

Critically Endangered at extremely high risk of becoming extinct in the wild, and meeting more of the criteria listed above than an endangered animal

Not Yet Evaluated scientists have not yet gathered enough information about the animal to determine whether it is threatened

Crustacean an animal without a backbone that has a hard exoskeleton and several pairs of jointed legs

Electroreception the ability to detect the tiny electrical impulses created by muscular contractions made by other animals

Esophagus a tube that connects the mouth to the stomach

Evergreen plants that keep their leaves year-round

Evolve to change over time. Animal species slowly change to be more suited to their habitats. This happens when individuals pass on helpful genes to their offspring.

Exoskeleton a series of hard plates that provide structure to the outside of a body

External on the outside

Extinct no longer existing; a species for which no animals are left alive

Gastropod a mollusk, such as a snail or slug, that has a single foot on its stomach

Habitat the kind of environment in which an animal is adapted to live

Forest an area covered in tall trees and smaller shrubs

Rain forest a forest of tall trees with a thick foliage, which receives at least 80 inches (200 cm) of rain a year

Desert an area, usually sandy and with few plants, that receives less than 10 inches (25 cm) of rain a year

Internal on the inside

Invertebrate an animal that does not have a backbone or skeleton. Many invertebrates have a hard exoskeleton that protects their bodies.

Lobe-finned fish a class of fish that hasn't evolved much over time. Lobe-finned fishes have fins that sit on stalks, rather than connecting directly to the body.

Mammal an animal that is warm-blooded, has some kind of fur or hair, and feeds its young milk produced by the mother

Mate to pair up with another animal of the same species in order to have babies

Mature full-grown

Mollusk an invertebrate with a soft body. Many invertebrates live in water and have shells.

Nematocysts special cells that sting, or deliver venom to, the skin of animals that brush against them

Notochord a flexible rod or chord that provides structure in certain animals. Many animals have notochords as embryos, but they grow into spinal cords as the embryos develop.

Parapodia flattened extensions on feet that are used as fins

Pore a tiny hole in the skin of an animal. Air and water can pass through pores.

Predator an animal that hunts and eats other animals

Prehensile able to be used for grabbing or holding objects

Prey an animal that is caught and eaten by a predator

Primates an order of mammals that includes humans, monkeys, and apes

Protrusion something that sticks out

Radula a ribbon, much like a tongue, that is covered in tiny teeth and used to tear pieces of food

Reptile an animal that is cold-blooded and has scales and usually lays eggs

Rhombus a shape that has four sides of equal length

Species a grouping of animals that is smaller than a class, in which the animals all share certain characteristics

Stridulation the production of sounds by rubbing together body parts

Ultrasonic vibrations sound that is too high-pitched to be heard by humans

Vertebrate an animal that is supported by a backbone and skeleton

definitions based on the 2001 IUCN Redlist Categories and Criteria version 3.1

EXPLORE SOME MORE

Scientists and conservationists around the world are working every day to learn more about animals—strange, unusual, gross, cool, and otherwise! You can learn more, too, by finding out about their work at these websites.

The International Union for Conservation of Nature (IUCN) is a group dedicated to helping conserve nature around the world. Its website at iucn.org includes articles about animals and habitats. The IUCN also publishes the IUCN Red List, a database of threatened animals. You can explore this searchable database at *iucnredlist.org.*

The World Wildlife Fund (WWF) is the largest conservation group in the world. It is working to save 40 species of animals by protecting the habitat where the animals live, educating the public about the animals, and working to change laws and policies that affect the environment. You can learn more about the animals and the environment at the WWF's website: *worldwildlife.org.*

The National Oceanic and Atmospheric Administration conducts research on subjects related to the ocean and weather, including the 2016 *Okeanos Explorer* expedition to the Mariana Trench. You can visit its website at *nmfs.noaa.gov.*

The Monterey Bay Aquarium, in California, works to protect oceans and ocean animals. Its website includes games, conservation information, and live web cams. You can start by learning about the animals in its animal guide at *montereybayaquarium. org/animal-guide.*

The National Zoo, in Washington, DC, is part of the Smithsonian Institution. It houses 1,800 animals, from 300 different species. You can tour its exhibits online and see photos and fact files of the animals at *nationalzoo.si.edu/animals.*

The Nature Conservancy protects unique habitats on five different continents. You can read about its preserves and conservation at *nature.org.*

The American Museum of Natural History explores science topics from evolution to astronomy to mineralogy to—you guessed it—animals. Visit its exploration page at *amnh.org/explore* to read articles and learn more about the exhibits at the museum.

More From Animal Planet

The Animal Planet website features videos, games, news, and information at *animalplanet.com.*

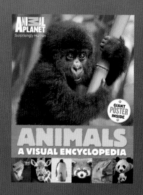

Animals: A Visual Encyclopedia

Meet more than 2,500 animals in this easy-to-use, photo-filled reference guide.

Animal Planet Animal Atlas

Travel around the world to explore different biomes and meet the animals that live in them through photographs, illustrations, and fascinating facts.

INDEX

Page numbers in **bold** refer to images.

PHOTO CREDITS

127

ACKNOWLEDGMENTS

Special thanks to the following experts, who took the time to review this material and provide feedback on its accuracy:

Michael Rentz, PhD
Lecturer, Iowa State University

Kevin J. McGowan, PhD
Cornell Lab of Ornithology

Andy Dehart
VP of Animal Husbandry
Patricia and Phillip Frost Museum of Science

Douglas L. Hotle
Professional Herpetologist

Brendan Dunphy
Zoologist
Iowa State University

Also thanks to the Discovery and Animal Planet Creative and Licensing teams: Denny Chen, Tracy Conner, Elizabeta Ealy, Robert Marick, Doris Miller, Sue Perez-Jackson, and Janet Tsuei